GOD, FREEDOM, AND IMMORTALITY

A Critical Analysis

GOD, FREEDOM, AND IMMORTALITY

A Critical Analysis

ANTONY FLEW

Prometheus Books

700 East Amherst St. Buffalo, New York 14215

Published 1984 by
Prometheus Books
700 E. Amherst Street, Buffalo, New York 14215
Printed in the United States of America

Copyright ©1984 by Antony Flew

First published as *The Presumption of Atheism* in 1976
in Great Britain by Elek Books Ltd. for Pemberton
Publishing Co. Ltd.

ISBN 0-87975-251-3
Library of Congress Catalog Card No. 84-42543

CONTENTS

INTRODUCTION

It has for years been a commonplace both of our serious Sundays and of our literary weeklies that philosophers who work in the English language are no longer concerned with great Kantian issues "of God, freedom and immortality". Certainly there have been, and are, many philosophers who would gladly—with appropriate professional alterations—rise to that legendary toast of the Trinity mathematicians: 'To pure mathematics; and may it never be of any use to anybody!' Nevertheless, as the title-page says, we have here a series of essays into this supposedly neglected philosophical territory.

The present book differs from most such composites in two ways. First, it is, even within the area specified, not a complete collection but rather a selection. It does not, for instance, include either short occasional contributions to the controversies provoked by 'Theology and Falsification' and 'Divine Omnipotence and Human Freedom', or any Critical Notices of books; or my long articles on 'Miracles' and 'Immortality' for *The Encyclopaedia of Philosophy*. Besides their obvious unity of subject and style, the essays chosen all exemplify the tactical approach made explicit in the first two chapters. Throughout I cleave to the Agnostic Principle, that we ought always to proportion our belief to the evidence. And, not only in Part One but also in Parts Two and Three, I insist that, wherever the argument may eventually lead, we should start by positioning ourselves as cautiously as can be upon the firmest and most universally familiar ground.

Second, although most of the present material has been somewhere in some form in print before, there was no question of idly sending a pile of offprints to the printers. For a start, I put whatever notes I could not manage to work smoothly into the text at the end, numbered consecutively throughout the whole volume; I compiled a single unified Bibliography, to include all works to which reference is made; and I inserted cross-references, and removed overlaps, between the chapters. I also imposed a uniform system both of sectioning and sub-sectioning, and of typographical conventions. (In particular I removed, even from passages quoted, all italics employed for purposes other than emphasis: the full naturalisation of such indispensable Latin immigrants as 'apriori' and 'aposteriori' is now centuries overdue, since they were first used in English—by Berkeley—over a quarter of a millennium ago!)

But as well as trying in these editorial ways to pull the various papers together, I have also more or less drastically revised, rearranged, and rewritten all the previously published material; so much so that in several cases it seemed proper to give fresh titles to the results. The bibliographical history is as follows:

'The Presumption of Atheism' was originally delivered as a lecture at the University of Arizona under the Howard W. Hintz Memorial Foundation. This article is reprinted, with comparatively minor revisions, from Volume II, Number 1 of the *Canadian Journal of Philosophy*, by permission of the Canadian Association for Publishing in Philosophy. 'The Principle of Agnosticism' is a more extensively revised version of 'Agnosticism', prepared for and published by *The Encyclopaedia Britannica*, 15th Edition, © 1974, Encyclopaedia Britannica, Inc. 'The Religious Hypothesis' first appeared in a shorter and rather rougher form in *The Rationalist Annual* for 1959. There is also some overlap between what appears here and Chapter IX of Flew (2), published by Routledge and Kegan Paul; but that chapter is far longer, and much more concerned with matters of Hume scholarship. 'What are Cosmological Arguments?' is a slightly modified version of 'The Cosmological Argument: A Terminological Suggestion', from *The Southwestern Journal of Philosophy* (Norman, Oklahoma), Volume II, Numbers 1 and 2, pp. 21–25, Spring 1971. 'Is Pascal's Wager the Only Safe Bet?' is a complete rewrite of what first burst out under the same title in 1956 in *The Rationalist Annual*, the predecessor of *Question*; sponsored by the Rationalist Press Association Ltd. of London. ' "Theology and Falsification": Silver Jubilee Review' is a new paper—except that it contains the original 'Theology and Falsification', first published in book form by the Student Christian Movement Press in Flew and MacIntyre (Ed.). 'The Free Will Defence' is based on 'Compatibilism, Free Will and God', published in *Philosophy* (London) for 1973. 'Philosophical Prolegomena to any Scientific Question of

Survival' is a not very extensively revised version of 'Is there a Case for Disembodied Survival?'. This originated as a lecture given in New York under the auspices of the American Society for Psychical Research. It was then published, somewhat expanded, in their *Journal* in April 1972. 'Can a Man Witness his own Funeral?' first appeared in 1956 in the now, alas, defunct *Hibbert Journal*; sponsored by the still, happily, active Hibbert Trust. 'The Identity of Incorporeal Persons' is a new paper, but it recycles some material taken from 'Locke and the Problem of Personal Identity', first published in *Philosophy* for 1951, and from ' "The Soul" of Mr A. M. Quinton', first published in *The Journal of Philosophy* (New York) for 1963. 'A Trinity of Temptations' is a virgin. 'What Does it Mean to Ask: "What is the Meaning of Life?" ' is a not all that much revised version of 'Tolstoi and the Meaning of Life', from *Ethics* (Chicago), published by the University of Chicago Press, in January 1963.

I thank all the various trusts, editors, and publishers for granting permissions to reuse this material here. Finally, I thank Mrs M. Quinlan, Secretary to the Department of Philosophy at Reading, for her help and patience in doing all the typing and photocopying needed to prepare this volume for the printers.

September 1975   A.F.

Part I
GOD

CHAPTER 1

The Presumption of Atheism

1. What it is, and why it matters

At the beginning of Book X of his last work *The Laws*, Plato turns his attention from violent and outrageous actions in general to the particular case of undisciplined and presumptuous behaviour in matters of religion:

> We have already stated summarily what the punishment should be for temple-robbing, whether by open force or secretly. But the punishments for the various sorts of insolence in speech or action with regard to the gods, which a man can show in word or deed, have to be proclaimed after we have provided an exordium. Let this be it: "No one believing, as the laws prescribe, in the existence of the gods has ever yet performed an impious action willingly, or uttered a lawless word. Anyone acting in such a way is in one of three conditions: either, first, he does not believe the proposition aforesaid; or, second, he believes that though the gods exist they have no concern about men; or, third, he believes that they can easily be won over by the bribery of prayer and sacrifice" (§885в).[1]

So Plato in this notorious treatment of heresy might be said to be rebuking the presumption of atheism. The word 'presumption' would then be employed as a synonym for 'presumptuousness'. But, despite the interest of the questions raised by Plato, the term has in my title a different interpretation. The presumption of atheism which I want to discuss is not a form of presumptuousness. Indeed it might be regarded as an expression of the very opposite, a modest teachability. My presumption of atheism is closely analogous to the presumption of innocence in the English law; a comparison which I shall develop in Section 2. What I want to examine is the contention that the debate about the existence of God should properly begin from the presumption of atheism, that the onus of proof must lie upon the theist.

The word 'atheism', however, has in this contention to be construed unusually. Whereas nowadays the usual meaning of 'atheist' in English is 'someone who asserts that there is no such being as God', I want the word to be understood not positively but negatively. I want the originally Greek prefix 'a' to be read in the same way in 'atheist' as it customarily is read in such other Greco-English words as 'amoral', 'atypical', and 'asymmetrical'. In this interpretation an atheist becomes: not someone who positively asserts the non-existence of God; but someone who is simply not a theist. Let us, for future ready reference, introduce the labels 'positive atheist' for the former and 'negative atheist' for the latter.

The introduction of this new interpretation of the word 'atheism' may appear to be a piece of perverse Humpty-Dumptyism, going arbitrarily against established common usage.[2] 'Whyever', it could be asked, 'don't you make it not the presumption of atheism but the presumption of agnosticism?' It is too soon to attempt a full answer to this challenge and this suggestion. My justification for introducing the notion of negative atheism will be found in the whole development of the present chapter. Then in Chapter Two I intend to argue for a return to the original usage of the word 'agnosticism', as first introduced by Thomas Henry Huxley. In the meantime it should be sufficient to point out that, following the present degenerate usage, an agnostic is one who, having entertained the proposition that God exists, now claims not to know either that it is or that it is not true. To be in this ordinary sense an agnostic you have already to have conceded that there is, and that you have, a legitimate concept of God; such that, whether or not this concept does in fact have application, it theoretically could. But the atheist in my peculiar interpretation, unlike the atheist in the usual sense, has not as yet and as such conceded even this.

This point is important, though the question whether the word 'agnosticism' could bear the meaning which I want now to give to the word 'atheism' is not. What the protagonist of my presumption of atheism wants to show is that the debate about the existence of God ought to be conducted in a particular way, and that the issue should be seen in a certain perspective. His thesis about the onus of proof involves that it is up to the theist: first, to introduce and to defend his proposed concept of God; and, second, to provide sufficient reason for believing that this concept of his does in fact have an application.

It is the first of these two stages which needs perhaps to be emphasised even more strongly than the second. Where the question of existence concerns, for instance, a Loch Ness Monster or an Abominable Snowman, this stage may perhaps reasonably be deemed to be more or less complete before the argument begins. But in the controversy about the existence of God this is certainly not so: not only for the quite familiar reason that the word 'God' is used—or misused—in many different ways; but also, and much more interestingly, because it cannot be taken for granted that even the would-be mainstream theist is operating with a legitimate concept which theoretically could have an application to an actual being.

This last suggestion is not really as new-fangled and factitious as it is sometimes thought to be. But its pedigree has been made a little hard to trace. For the fact is that, traditionally, issues which should be seen as concerning the legitimacy or otherwise of a proposed or supposed concept have by philosophical theologians been discussed, either as surely disposable difficulties in reconciling one particular feature of the Divine nature with another, or else as aspects of an equally surely soluble general problem of saying something about the infinite Creator in language intelligible to His finite creatures. These traditional and still almost universally accepted forms of presentation are fundamentally prejudicial. For they assume that there is a Divine Being, with an actual nature the features of which we can investigate. They assume that there is an Infinite Creator, whose existence—whatever difficulties we finite creatures may have in asserting anything else about Him—we may take for granted.

The general reason why this presumption of atheism matters is that its acceptance must put the whole question of the existence of God into an entirely fresh perspective. Most immediately relevant here is that in this fresh perspective problems which really are conceptual are seen as conceptual

problems; and problems which have tended to be regarded as
advanced and, so to speak, optional extras now discover
themselves as both elementary and indispensable. The theist
who wants to build a systematic and thorough apologetic finds
that he is required to begin absolutely from the beginning. This
absolute beginning is to ensure that the word 'God' is provided
with a meaning such that it is theoretically possible for an actual
being to be so described.

Although I shall later be arguing that the presumption of
atheism is neutral as between all parties to the main dispute, in
as much as to accept it as determining a procedural framework
is not to make any substantive assumptions, I must give fair
warning now that I do nevertheless believe that in its fresh
perspective the whole enterprise of theism appears even more
difficult and precarious than it did before. In part this is a
corollary of what I have just been suggesting; that certain
difficulties and objections, which may previously have seemed
peripheral or even factitious, are made to stand out as fundamental and unavoidable. But it is also in part, as we shall be
seeing soon, a consequence of the emphasis which it places on
the imperative need to produce some sort of sufficient reason to
justify theist belief.

2. The presumption of atheism and the presumption of innocence
One thing which helps to conceal this need is a confusion about
the possible varieties of proof, and this confusion is one which
can be resolved with the help of the first of a series of
comparisons between my proposed presumption of atheism and
the legal presumption of innocence.

(i) It is frequently said nowadays, even by professing Roman
Catholics, that everyone knows that it is impossible to prove the
existence of God. The first objection to this putative truism is,
as my reference to Roman Catholics should have suggested, that
it is not true. For it is an essential dogma of Roman Catholicism,
defined as such by the First Vatican Council, that "the one and
true God our creator and lord can be known for certain
through the creation by the natural light of human reason"
(Denzinger, §1806). So even if this dogma is, as I myself
believe, false, it is certainly not known to be false by those many
Roman Catholics who remain, despite all the disturbances

consequent upon the Second Vatican Council, committed to the complete traditional faith.

To this a sophisticated objector might reply that the definition of the First Vatican Council speaks of knowing for certain rather than of proving or demonstrating; adding perhaps, if he was very sophisticated indeed, that the word 'demonstrari' in an earlier draft was eventually replaced by the expression 'certo cognosci'. But, allowing that this is correct, it is certainly not enough to vindicate the conventional wisdom. For the word 'proof' is not ordinarily restricted in its application to demonstratively valid arguments, that is, in which the conclusion cannot be denied without thereby contradicting the premises. So it is too flattering to suggest that most of those who make this facile claim, that everyone knows that it is impossible to prove the existence of God, are intending only the strictly limited assertion that one special sort of proof, demonstrative proof, is impossible.

The truth, and the danger, is that wherever there is any awareness of such a limited and specialised interpretation, there will be a quick and illegitimate move to the much wider general conclusion that it is impossible and, furthermore, unnecessary to provide any sufficient reason for believing. It is, therefore, worth underlining that when the presumption of atheism is explained as insisting that the onus of proof must be on the theist, the word 'proof' is being used in the ordinary wide sense in which it can embrace any and every variety of sufficient reason. It is, of course, in this and only this sense that the word is interpreted when the presumption of innocence is explained as laying the onus of proof on the prosecution.

(ii) A second element of positive analogy between these two presumptions is that both are defeasible; and that they are, consequently, not to be identified with assumptions. The presumption of innocence indicates where the court should start and how it must proceed. Yet the prosecution is still able, more often than not, to bring forward what is in the end accepted as sufficient reason to warrant the verdict 'Guilty'; which appropriate sufficient reason is properly characterised as a proof of guilt. The defeasible presumption of innocence is thus in this majority of cases in fact defeated. Were the indefeasible innocence of all accused persons an assumption of any legal system, then there could not be within that system any provision for any verdict other than 'Not Guilty'. To the extent that it is, for instance, an assumption of the English Common Law that every citizen is cognisant of all that the law requires of him, that law cannot admit the fact that this assumption is, as in fact it is, false.

The presumption of atheism is similarly defeasible. It lays it down that thorough and systematic inquiry must start from a position of negative atheism, and that the burden of proof lies on the theist proposition. Yet this is not at all the same thing as demanding that the debate should proceed on either a positive or a negative atheist assumption, which must preclude a theist conclusion. Counsel for theism no more betrays his client by accepting the framework determined by this presumption than counsel for the prosecution betrays the state by conceding the legal presumption of innocence. The latter is perhaps in his heart unshakably convinced of the guilt of the defendant. Yet he must, and with complete consistency and perfect sincerity may, insist that the proceedings of the court should respect the presumption of innocence. The former is even more likely to be persuaded of the soundness of his brief. Yet he too can with a good conscience allow that a thorough and complete apologetic must start from, meet, and go on to defeat, the presumption of atheism.

Put as I have just been putting it, the crucial distinction between a defeasible presumption and a categorical assumption will, no doubt, seem quite obvious. But obviousness really is, what some other things nowadays frequently said to be are not, essentially relative: what is obvious to one person at one time may not have been obvious to that same person at an earlier time, and may not be obvious now to another. There is no doubt but that many do find the present distinction difficult to grasp, especially in its application to exciting cases. Indeed one reason why I decided to write the lecture on which the present chapter is based is that I had found even the most acute and sympathetic critics of my *God and Philosophy* faulting me for asking everyone to start from my own notoriously atheist assumptions. It was clear that a more lucid and more adequately argued statement was needed. For in that book I had recommended only the present methodological presumption, not a substantive assumption.

I cite another example from a quite different sphere, an example which is again the more salutary since the offender was above suspicion of any dishonourable intent wilfully to misunderstand or misrepresent. Lord Attlee, once Leader of the British Labour Party, reproached the "general assumption that all applicants are frauds unless they prove themselves otherwise" (Young and Ashton, p. 111). But, we must insist, to put the onus of proof of entitlement upon the beneficiary is not to assume that all, or most, or even any of those who apply for welfare benefits are in fact cheats. Such presumptions are procedural purely. They assume no substantive conclusions.

(iii) However—and here we come to a third element in the positive analogy—to say that such presumptions are in themselves procedural and not substantive is not to say that the higher-order questions of whether to follow this presumption or that are trifling and merely formal rather than material and substantial. These higher-order questions are not questions which can be dismissed cynically as 'issues of principle as opposed to issues of substance'. It can matter a lot which presumption is adopted. Notoriously there is a world of difference between legal systems which follow the presumption of innocence, and those which do not. And, as I began to indicate at the end of Section 1, to adopt the presumption of atheism does put the whole argument into a distinctive perspective.

(iv) Next, as a fourth element in the positive analogy, it is a paradoxical consequence of the fact that these presumptions are procedural and not substantive that particular defeats do not constitute any sort of reason, much less a sufficient reason, for a general surrender. The fact that George Joseph Smith was in his trial proved guilty of many murders defeats the original presumption of his innocence. But this particular defeat has no tendency at all to show that even in this particular case the court should not have proceeded on this presumption. Still less does it tend to establish that the legal system as a whole was at fault in incorporating this presumption as a general principle. It is the same with the presumption of atheism. Suppose that someone is able to prove the existence of God. This achievement must, similarly, defeat our presumption. But it does not thereby show that the original contention about the onus of proof was mistaken.

Etymologically the word 'defeasible' (= defeatable) does imply precisely this capacity of survive defeat. A substantive generalisation—such as, for instance, the assertion that all persons accused of murder are in fact innocent—is falsified decisively by the production of even one authentic counter-example. But a defeasible presumption is not shown to have been the wrong one to have made by being in a particular case in fact defeated.

3. The case for the presumption of atheism

What does show the presumption of atheism to be the right one is what we have now to investigate.

(i) An obvious first move is to appeal to the old legal axiom: "Ei incumbit probatio qui dicit, non qui negat." Literally and unsympathetically translated this becomes: "The onus of proof lies on the man who affirms, not on the man who denies." To this the objection is almost equally obvious. Given just a very little verbal ingenuity, the content of any motion can be rendered alternatively in either a negative or a positive form: either, "That this house denies the existence of God"; or, "That this house takes its stand for positive atheism". So interpreted, therefore, our axiom provides no determinate guidance.[3]

Suppose, however, that we take the hint already offered in the previous paragraph. A less literal but more sympathetic translation would be: "The onus of proof lies on the proposition, not on the opposition." The point of the change is to bring out that this maxim was offered in a legal context, and that our courts are institutions of debate. An axiom providing no determinate guidance outside that framework may nevertheless be fundamental for the effective conduct of orderly and decisive debate. Here the outcome is supposed to be decided on the merits of what is said within the debate itself, and of that alone. So no opposition can set about demolishing the proposition case until and unless that proposition has first provided them with a case for demolition: "You've got to get something on your plate before you can start messing it around" (Austin (2), p. 142).

Of course our maxim even when thus sympathetically interpreted still offers no direction on which contending parties ought to be made to undertake which roles. Granting that courts are to operate as debating institutions, and granting that this maxim is fundamental to debate, we have to appeal to some further premise principle before we become licensed to infer that the prosecution must propose and the defence oppose. This further principle is, once again, the familiar presumption of innocence. Were we, while retaining the conception of a court as an institution for reaching decisions by way of formalised debate, to embrace the opposite presumption, the presumption of guilt, we should need to adopt the opposite arrangements. In these the defence would first propose that the accused is after all innocent, and the prosecution would then respond by struggling to disintegrate the case proposed.

(ii) The first move examined cannot, therefore, be by itself sufficient. To have considered it does nevertheless help to show that to accept such a presumption is to adopt a policy. And policies have to be assessed by reference to the aims of those for whom they are suggested. If for you it is more important that no guilty person should ever be acquitted than that no innocent person should ever be convicted, then for you a presumption of guilt must be the rational policy. For you, with your preference structure, a presumption of innocence becomes simply irrational. To adopt this policy would be to adopt means calculated to frustrate your own chosen ends; which is, surely, paradigmatically irrational. Take, as an actual illustration, the controlling elite of a ruling Leninist party, which must as such refuse to recognise any individual rights if these conflict with the claims of the party, and which in fact treats all those suspected of actual or potential opposition much as if they were already known 'counter-revolutionaries', 'enemies of socialism', 'friends of the United States', 'advocates of free elections', and all other like things bad. I can, and do, fault this policy and its agents on many counts. Yet I cannot say that for them, once granted their scale of values, it is irrational.

What then are the aims by reference to which an atheist presumption might be justified? One key word in the answer, if not the key word, must be 'knowledge'. The context for which such a policy is proposed is that of inquiry about the existence of

God; and the object of the exercise is, presumably, to discover whether it is possible to establish that the word 'God' does in fact have application. Now to establish must here be either to show that you know or to come to know. But knowledge is crucially different from mere true belief. All knowledge involves true belief; not all true belief constitutes knowledge. To have a true belief is simply and solely to believe that something is so, and to be in fact right. But someone may believe that this or that is so, and his belief may in fact be true, without its thereby and necessarily constituting knowledge. If a true belief is to achieve this more elevated status, then the believer has to be properly warranted so to believe. He must, that is, be in a position to know.

Obviously there is enormous scope for disagreement in particular cases: both about what is required in order to be in a position to know; and about whether these requirements have actually been satisfied. But the crucial distinction between believing truly and knowing is recognised as universally as the prior and equally vital distinction between believing and believing what is in fact true. If, for instance, there is a question whether a colleague performed some discreditable action, then all of us, though we have perhaps to admit that we cannot help believing that he did, are rightly scrupulous not to assert that this is known unless we have grounds sufficient to warrant the bolder claim. It is, therefore, not only incongruous but also scandalous in matters of life and death, and even of eternal life and death, to maintain that you know either on no grounds at all, or on grounds of a kind which on other and comparatively minor issues you yourself would insist to be inadequate.

It is by reference to this inescapable demand for grounds that the presumption of atheism is justified. If it is to be established that there is a God, then we have to have good grounds for believing that this is indeed so. Until and unless some such grounds are produced we have literally no reason at all for believing; and in that situation the only reasonable posture must be that of either the negative atheist or the agnostic. So the onus of proof has to rest on the proposition. It must be up to them: first, to give whatever sense they choose to the word 'God', meeting any objection that so defined it would relate only to an incoherent pseudo-concept; and, second, to bring forward sufficient reasons to warrant their claim that, in their present sense of the word 'God', there is a God. The same applies, with appropriate alterations, if what is to be made out is, not that theism is known to be true, but only—more modestly—that it can be seen to be at least more or less probable.

4. Objections to the presumption of atheism

Once the nature of this presumption is understood, the supporting case is, as we have just seen in Section 3, short and simple.

(i) One reason why it may appear unacceptable is a confusion of contexts. In a theist or post-theist society it comes more easily to ask why a man is not a theist than why he is. Provided that the question is to be construed biographically this is no doubt methodologically inoffensive. But our concern here is not all with biographical questions of why people came to hold whatever opinions they do hold. Rather it is with the need for opinions to be suitably grounded if they are to be rated as items of knowledge, or even of probable belief. The issue is: not what does or does not need to be explained biographically; but where the burden of theological proof should rest.

(ii) A more sophisticated objection of fundamentally the same sort would urge that our whole discussion has been too artificial and too general, and that any man's enquiries have to begin from wherever he happens to be: "We cannot begin with complete doubt. We must begin with all the prejudices which we actually have. . . . These prejudices are not to be dispelled by a maxim" (Peirce, Volume V, pp. 156–157). Professor John Hick has urged, in *Theology Today* for 1967: "The right question is whether it is rational for the religious man himself, given that his religious experience is coherent, persistent, and compelling, to affirm the reality of God. What is in question is not the rationality of an inference from certain psychological events to God as their cause; for the religious man no more infers the existence of God than we infer the existence of the visible world around us. What is in question is the rationality of the one who has the religious experiences. If we regard him as a rational person we must acknowledge that he is rational in believing what, given his experiences, he cannot help believing" (Hick, *loc. cit.*, pp. 86–87).

To the general point drawn from Peirce the answer comes from further reading of Peirce himself. He was in the paper from which I quoted arguing against the Cartesian programme of simultaneous, systematic, and (almost) universal doubt. Peirce did not want to suggest that it is impossible or wrong to subject any of our beliefs to critical scrutiny. In the same paragraph he continues: "A person may, it is true, find reason to doubt what he began by believing; but in that case he doubts because he has a positive reason for it, and not on account of the Cartesian maxim." One positive reason for being especially leery towards religious opinions is that these vary so very much from society to society; being, it seems, mainly determined, as Descartes has it, "by custom and example". The phrase occurs, in Part II of his *Discourse on the Method*, almost immediately after the observation: "I took into account also the very different character which a person brought up from infancy in France or Germany exhibits, from that which . . . he would have possessed had he lived among the Chinese or with savages."

To Hick it has at once to be conceded: that it is one thing to say that a belief is unfounded or well-founded; and quite another to say that it is irrational or rational for some particular person, in his particular time and circumstances, and with his particular experience and lack of experience, to hold or to reject that belief. Granted that his usually reliable Intelligence were sure that the enemy tank brigade was in the town, it was entirely reasonable for the General also to believe this. But the enemy tanks had in fact pulled back. Yet it was still unexceptionably sensible for the General on his part to refuse to expose his flank to those tanks which were in fact not there. This genuine and important distinction cannot, however, save the day for Hick.

In the first place, to show that someone may reasonably hold a particular belief, and even that he may properly claim that he knows it to be true, is at best still not to show that that belief is indeed well-grounded, much less that it constitutes an item of his knowledge.

Nor, second, is to accept the presumption of atheism as a methodological framework, as such: either to deprive anyone of his right "to affirm the reality of God"; or to require that to be respectable every conviction should first have been reached through the following of an ideally correct procedure. To insist on the correctness of this presumption as an initial presumption is to make a claim which is itself procedural rather than substantive; and the context for which this particular procedure is being recommended is that of justification rather than of discovery.

Once these fundamentals are appreciated, those for whom Hick is acting as spokesman should at first feel quite content. For on his account they consider that they have the very best of grounds for their beliefs. They regard their "coherent, consistent, and compelling" religious experience as analogous to perception; and the man who can see something with his own eyes and feel it in his own hands is in a perfect position to know that it exists. His position is indeed so perfect that, as Hick says, it is wrong to speak here of evidence and inference. If he saw his wife in the act of intercourse with a lover then he no longer needs to infer her infidelity from bits and pieces of evidence. He has now what is better than inference; although for the rest of us, who missed this display, his testimony still constitutes an important part of the evidence in the case. The idiomatic expression, 'the evidence of my own eyes', derives its paradoxical piquancy from the fact that to see for oneself is better than to have evidence (Austin (2), pp. 115–116).

All this is true. Certainly, too, anyone who thinks that he can as it were see God must reject the suggestion that is so doing he infers "from certain psychological events to God as their cause". For to accept this account would be to call down upon his head all the insoluble difficulties which fall to the lot of all those who maintain that what we see, and all we ever really and directly see, is visual sense-data. And, furthermore, it is useful to be reminded that when we insist that knowledge as opposed to mere belief has to be adequately warranted, this grounding may be a matter either of having sufficient evidence or of being in a position to know directly and without evidence. So far, therefore it might seem that Hick's objection was completely at cross-purposes; and that anyway his protégés have no need to appeal to the distinction between actual knowledge and what one may rationally and properly claim to know.

Wait a minute. The passage of Hick which has been under discussion was part of an attempt to show that criticism of the Argument from Religious Experience is irrelevant to such claims to as it were see God. But on the contrary: what such criticism usually challenges is just the vital assumption that having religious experience really is a kind of perceiving, and hence a sort of being in a position to know about its putative object. So this challenge provides just exactly that positive reason, which Peirce demanded, for doubting what, according to Hick, "one who has the religious experiences . . . cannot help believing". If therefore he persists in so believing, without even attempting to overcome this criticism, then it becomes impossible to vindicate his claims to be harbouring rational beliefs; much less items of authentic knowledge.

(iii) A third objection, of a different kind, starts from the assumption, mentioned already in Section 2 (i), that any programme to prove the existence of God is fundamentally misconceived; that this enterprise is on all fours with projects to square the circle or to construct a perpetual motion machine. The suggestion then is that the territory which reason cannot inhabit may nevertheless be freely colonised by faith: "Faith alone can take you forward, when reason has gone as far as it can go"; and so on.

Ultimately perhaps it is impossible to establish the existence of God, or even to show that it is more or less probable. But, if so, this is not the correct moral: the rational man does not thereby become in this area free to believe, or not to believe, just as his fancy takes him. Faith, surely, should not be a leap in the dark but a leap towards the light. Arbitrarily to plump for some particular conviction, and then stubbornly to cleave to it, would be—to borrow the term which Thomas Aquinas employed in discussing faith, reason and revelation in the *Summa contra Gentiles*—'frivolous' (I(vi): his Latin word is 'levis').[4] If your venture of faith is not to be arbitrary, irrational, and frivolous, you must have presentable reasons: first for making any such commitment in this area, an area in which by hypothesis the available grounds are insufficient to warrant any firm conclusion; and second for opting for one particular possibility rather than any of the other available alternatives. To most such offerings of reasons the presumption of atheism remains relevant. For though, again by the hypothesis, these cannot aspire to prove their conclusions they will usually embrace some estimation of their probability. If the onus of proof lies on the man who hopes definitively to establish the existence of God, it must also by the same token rest on the person who plans to make out only that this conclusion is more or less probable.

I put in the qualifications 'most' and 'usually' in order to allow for apologetic in the tradition of Pascal's Wager, which I shall discuss more fully in Chapter Five. Pascal makes no attempt in this most famous argument to show that his Roman Catholicism is true or probably true. The reasons which he suggests for making the recommended bet on his particular faith are reasons in the sense of motives rather than reasons in our previous sense of grounds. Conceding, if only for the sake of the present argument, that we can have no knowledge here, Pascal tries to justify as prudent a policy of systematic self-persuasion, rather than to provide grounds for thinking that the beliefs recommended are actually true.

5. The Five Ways as an attempt to defeat the presumption of atheism

I have tried, in the first four sections of this chapter, to explain what I mean by 'the presumption of atheism', to bring out by comparison with the presumption of innocence in law what such a presumption does and does not involve, to deploy a case for adopting my presumption of atheism, and to indicate the lines on which two sorts of objection may be met. Now, finally, I want to point out that Thomas Aquinas presented the Five Ways in his *Summa Theologica* as an attempt to defeat just such a presumption. My hope in this is, both to draw attention to something which seems generally to be overlooked, and by so doing to summon a massive authority in support of a thesis which many apparently find scandalous.

These most famous arguments were offered there originally, without any inhibition or equivocation, as proofs, period: "I reply that we must say that God can be proved in five ways"; and the previous second Article, raising the question "Whether the existence of God can be demonstrated?", gives the categorical affirmative answer that "the existence of God . . . can be demonstrated" (I Q2 A3). It is worth stressing this point, since it is frequently denied. Thus, for instance, in an article in *Philosophy* for 1968, Dr L. C. Velecky asserts, without citation or compunction: "He did not prove here the existence of God, nor indeed, did he prove it anywhere else, for a very good reason. According to Thomas, God's existence is unknowable and, hence, cannot be proved" (p. 226). The quotations just made from Aquinas ought to be decisive. Yet there seems to be quite a school of devout interpretation which waves aside what Aquinas straightforwardly said as almost irrelevant to the question of what he really meant.

Attention usually and understandably concentrates on the main body of the third Article, which is the part where Aquinas gives his five supposed proofs. But, as so often, it is rewarding to read the entire Article, and especially the second of the two Objections to which these are presented as a reply: "Furthermore, what can be accounted for by fewer principles is not the product of more. But it seems that everything which can be observed in the world can be accounted for by other principles, on the assumption of the non-existence of God. Thus natural effects are explained by natural causes, while contrived effects are referred to human reason and will. So there is no need to postulate the existence of God."

(i) The Five Ways are thus at least in one aspect an attempt to defeat this presumption of (an Aristotelian) atheist naturalism, by showing that the things "which can be observed in the world" cannot "be accounted for . . . on the assumption of the non-existence of God", and hence that there is "need to postulate the existence of God".

In this perspective it becomes easier to see why Aquinas makes so much use of Aristotelian scientific ideas in his arguments. That these are in fact much more dependent than is often realised on those now largely obsolete ideas is usefully emphasised in Anthony Kenny's *The Five Ways*. But Kenny does not bring out that they were deployed against a presumption of atheist naturalism.

Also one must never forget that Aquinas composed his own Objections, and hence that it was he who introduced into his formulation here the idea of (this Aristotelian) scientific naturalism. No such idea is integral to the presumption of atheism as that has been construed in the present paper. When the addition is made the presumption can perhaps be labelled Stratonician. (Strato was the next but one in succession to Aristotle as head of the Lyceum, and was regarded by Bayle and Hume as the archetypal ancient spokesman for an atheist scientific naturalism.)

By suggesting, a century before Ockham, an appeal to an Ockhamist principle of postulational economy Aquinas also indicates a reason for adopting such a presumption. The fact that Aquinas cannot be suspected of wanting to reach any sort of atheist conclusions can now be made to serve as a spectacular illustration of a point laboured in Section 2, that to adopt such a presumption is not to make an assumption. And the fact which has been put forward as an objection to this reading of Aquinas, that "Thomas himself was never in the position of a Stratonician, nor did he live in a milieu in which Stratonicians were plentiful" (Velecky, *op. cit.*, pp. 225–226), is simply irrelevant. For the thesis that the onus of proof lies upon the theist is entirely independent of these historical and social facts. It is in the perspective provided by that thesis—a thesis apparently accepted by Aquinas himself—that we shall examine in Chapter Three and Chapter Five two famous attempts to defeat the presumption.

(ii) What is perhaps slightly awkward for present purposes is the formulation of the first Objection: "It seems that God does not exist. For if of two contrary things one were to exist without limit the other would be totally eliminated. But what is meant by this word 'God' is something good without limit. So if God were to have existed no evil would have been encountered. But evil is encountered in the world. Therefore, God does not exist."

It would from my point of view have been better had this first Objection referred to possible difficulties and incoherencies in the meaning proposed for the word 'God'. Unfortunately it does not, although Aquinas is elsewhere acutely aware of such problems. The changes required, however, are, though important, not extensive. Certainly, the Objection as actually given is presented as one of the God hypothesis falsified by familiar fact. Yet a particular variety of the same general point could be represented as the detection of an incoherence, not in the proposed concept of God as such, but between that concept and another element in the theoretical structure in which it is normally involved.

The incoherence—or perhaps on this occasion I should say only the ostensible incoherence—is between the idea of creation, as necessarily involving complete, continual and absolute dependence of creature upon Creator, and the idea that creatures may nevertheless be sufficiently autonomous for their faults not to be also and indeed primarily His fault. The former idea, the idea of creation, is so essential that it provides the traditional criterion for distinguishing theism from deism. The latter is no less central to the three great theist systems of Judaism, Christianity, and Islam, since all three equally insist that creatures of the immaculate Creator are corrupted by sin. So where Aquinas put as his first Objection a statement of the traditional Problem of Evil, conceived as a problem of squaring the God hypothesis with certain undisputed facts, a redactor fully seized of the presumption of atheism as expounded in the present paper would refer instead to the ostensible incoherence, within the system itself, between the concept of creation by a flawless Creator and the notion of His creatures flawed by their sins. As for whether this incoherence is not only ostensible but also actual I shall have something to say in Chapter Seven.

CHAPTER 2

The Principle of Agnosticism

At the beginning of the previous chapter I distinguished a new negative sense of the word 'atheism'. The remainder provided, among other things, justification for that innovation. I now want not to distinguish a new sense of the word 'agnosticism', but to revive its old original interpretation. The methodological presumption of atheism, reinforced by a complementary insistence upon this principle of agnosticism, may perhaps define sufficiently the firm yet undogmatic posture in which I propose to approach questions of religious belief.

1. What it is

The word 'Agnosticism' was first introduced, as a suitable label for his own position, by that great Victorian T. H. Huxley: "It came into my head as suggestively antithetical to the 'Gnostic' of Church history, who professed to know so much about the very things of which I was ignorant" (Huxley (2), Volume V, p. 239).

(i) This first statement brings out that Agnosticism in his sense—to which I grant the distinction of an initial capital—is something to do with not knowing, and that this not knowing refers especially to the sphere of religious doctrine. Etymology, however, and now common usage, do permit a less limited employment of the term. V. I. Lenin, for instance, in his *Materialism and Empirio-Criticism* recognised, as attempted half-way houses between true red-blooded materialism and the equally uninhibited idealism of George Berkeley, the 'agnosticisms' of David Hume and Immanuel Kant; which in the present context consisted in their contentions about the unknowability of the nature, or even the existence, of 'things-in-themselves'.

Agnosticism in its primary reference is commonly contrasted with atheism: "The atheist asserts that there is no God, whereas the agnostic maintains only that he does not know." This common contrast is here in two respects misleading. First: Huxley himself certainly rejected as outright false rather than as not known to be true (or false) many widely popular views about God, His providence, and our posthumous destiny. Second: if this were crucial, Agnosticism would for almost all practical purposes be the same as atheism. It was indeed on this misunderstanding that Huxley and his associates were attacked both by enthusiastic Christian polemicists and by Friedrich Engels as "shamefaced atheists" (quoted by Lenin, p. 211). This harsh description is indeed well merited by many of those who nowadays prefer to adopt what is felt to be the more comfortable label.

But the essence of Huxley's Agnosticism is something proud and positive; and his interpretation, as the original promoter of the term, must be peculiarly authoritative. Huxley's Agnosticism is not a profession of total nescience, or even of total nescience within one special but very large sphere. Rather, he insisted, it was "not a creed but a method, the essence of which lies in the rigorous application of a single principle" (Huxley (2), Volume V, p. 245). This principle is to follow reason "as far as it can take you"; but then, when you have established as much as you can, frankly and honestly to recognise the limits of your knowledge.

It is the same principle as that proclaimed later by the mathematician and philosopher W. K. Clifford in his luminous and compulsive essay, 'The Ethics of Belief'. Clifford works with the example of a shipowner allowing an emigrant ship to go to sea when it was in fact unseaworthy; arguing that neither the sincerity nor even the disinterestedness of a belief that the ship was seaworthy is adequate excuse for believing against the weight of the available evidence: "It is wrong always, every-where, and for everyone, to believe anything on insufficient evidence" (Clifford, p. 346).

Applied by Huxley to the incomparably more important matter of fundamental Christian claims, this principle yields characteristically sceptical conclusions: "One may suspect that a little more critical discrimination would have enlarged the

Apocrypha not inconsiderably" (Huxley (2), Volume V, p. 224).
In the same spirit Sir Leslie Stephen, in *An Agnostic's Apology*,
reproaches those who pretend to delineate "the nature of God
Almighty with an accuracy from which modest naturalists
would shrink in describing the genesis of a black beetle"
(Stephen, p. 4).

(ii) Agnosticism, however, is not the same as Scepticism.
This, in the comprehensive and Classical form epitomised by
Sextus Empiricus, confidently challenges not just religious or
metaphysical but all knowledge claims venturing beyond
immediate experience. Agnosticism is, what such Classical
Scepticism surely could not be, compatible with a Positivist
emphasis on the achievements and possibilities of natural and
social science; whatever reserves most Agnostics may harbour
about the more authoritarian and eccentric features of the
system of Auguste Comte. (Huxley himself was certainly
representative when he ridiculed "the incongruous mixture of
bad science with eviscerated papistry, out of which Comte
manufactured the Positivist religion"; and characterised
Comte's works as, simply, "repulsive" (Huxley (2), Volume V,
p. 255).)

(iii) It is also possible to speak of a religious Agnosticism. But
if this expression is not to be contradictory it has to be taken to
refer to an acceptance of the Agnostic Principle, with either a
conviction that at least some minimum of affirmative religious
doctrine can be established on adequate grounds, or else a
devotion to the sort of religion or religiousness which makes no
very substantial or disputatious doctrinal demands.

Huxley himself allowed for the possibility of consistently
combining Agnosticism with substantive religious beliefs which
he himself rejected as false, or unwarranted, or both. Thus he
contrasts "scientific Theology", with which "Agnosticism has
no quarrel", with "Ecclesiasticism, or, as our neighbours across
the Channel call it, Clericalism"; and his complaint against
these is not that they reach substantive conclusions different
from his own but that they maintain "that it is morally wrong
not to believe certain propositions, whatever the results of
strict scientific investigation of the evidence of these propositions" (Huxley (2), Volume V, p. 313).

The second possibility, that of an Agnosticism which is

c

religious but involves precious little in the way of religious beliefs, was realised perhaps most strikingly in the Buddha. Typically and traditionally, the Ecclesiastical Christian has insisted that absolute certainty about some minimum approved list of propositions concerning God and the general Divine scheme of things is wholly necessary to salvation. Equally typically, the Buddha side-stepped all such speculative questions. At best they could only distract attention from the urgent business of salvation—salvation, of course, in his own very different interpretation.

2. Historical antecedents of modern Agnosticism

The ancestry of modern secular and atheist Agnosticism in Europe may be traced back to the Greek Sophists and to Socrates: not, of course, the 'Socrates' of Plato's *Republic*—the would-be Founding Father of a supposedly ideal and certainly totalitarian state; but the shadowy historical Socrates—said to have been hailed by the Oracle of Delphi as the wisest of men because he knew what, and how much, he did not know. But the most important and immediate source of such Agnostic ideas was surely Hume; while Hume's successor Kant—the second of the two great philosophers of the Age of Enlightenment—may well be seen as the prime philosophical inspirer of religious reactions against them.

(i) Huxley, as we have seen, demanded that we should, as a matter of positive principle, recognise and accept the limits of our knowledge. In taking it that these limits embrace neither the findings of a general natural theology nor the contents of a particular special Divine revelation, Huxley was also accepting a Humian critique of the putative rational foundations of both natural and revealed religion. (Huxley's was the most sympathetic book on Hume to be published in Huxley's century.) Hume's undermining is in his *Inquiry concerning Human Understanding* and in the posthumous *Dialogues concerning Natural Religion*. This first *Inquiry* attempts—in the tradition of the earlier *Essay concerning Human Understanding* of John Locke and of Kant's *Critique of Pure Reason* later—to determine the limits of our possible knowledge.

Two sections refer directly: that 'Of Miracles'; and that 'Of a Particular Providence and of a Future State'. In the latter

Hume starts from his basic empiricist claims: that, generally, "matters of fact and real existence" cannot be known apriori; and that, particularly, we cannot know apriori that any thing or kind of thing either must be or cannot be the cause of any other thing or kind of thing. This disposes of all the classical arguments other than the Argument to Design. Hume's treatment of that is the subject of Chapter Three. Later, in his *Dialogues*, Hume develops Strato's suggestion that whatever order we discover in the Universe should be attributed not to some specially postulated outside Cause but to the Universe itself; a suggestion already mentioned in Section 5(i) of Chapter One.

In the other of these two sections Hume takes his stand on Agnostic principle: "A wise man . . . proportions his belief to the evidence." Like all his contemporaries, he conceives a miracle as a "violation of a law of nature". Only such an overriding of a strong natural order could give us good reason to believe that a Power greater than Nature was thereby endorsing the claims of some putative revelation. Hume's contribution is methodological. He contends that the principles and presuppositions upon which the critical historian must rely, in first interpreting the detritus of the past as historical evidence, and then building up from this his account of what actually happened, are such as to make it impossible for him "to prove a miracle and make it a just foundation for any such system of religion".[5]

In this two-pronged attack Hume challenged what was in his day, and long remained, the standard framework for systematic rational apologetic. Indeed the contrary contentions were in 1870–71 defined as essential and constitutive dogmas of Roman Catholicism by decrees of the First Vatican Council. This anathematised both those who deny the possibility of developing a framework of natural theology, and those who deny the possibility of establishing the authenticity of a supplementary revelation by proving the occurrence of endorsing miracles (Denzinger, §§1806 and 1813, respectively).

(ii) With an eye to what was to follow, it has to be emphasised that Hume's official position, like Kant's, was that knowledge in this area is practically impossible. This thesis is stronger than that of those who simply confess that they just do not know. Consider, as an example of such unsophisticated nescience, Aboriginals of the Northern Territories of Australia singing:

> The God-men say when die go sky
> Through pearly gates where river flow,
> The God-men say when die we fly
> Just like eagle, hawk and crow—
> Might be, might be; I don't know.[6]

Yet Hume's thesis was still weaker than that of his neo-Humian successors, the Logical Positivists of the Vienna Circle. They maintained that any talk about a transcendent God must be "without literal significance". This view was presented brilliantly, and in an uncompromisingly drastic form, by A. J. Ayer in his juvenile masterpiece *Language, Truth and Logic*. Similar conclusions were reached less high-handedly but with less panache by contributors to *New Essays in Philosophical Theology* (Flew and MacIntyre (Eds.), pp. 187–211).

(iii) Looking backwards, we can now see—what he himself did not know—that Hume's attack on the possibility of a positive natural theology had to a considerable extent been anticipated by fourteenth-century Christian Scholastics: generally by William of Ockham; and with particular reference to the lack of apriori knowledge of causal relations by Nicolas of Autrecourt. (No one, it seems, had told them that the belief in the possibility of natural theology was going to become an essential of their religion.)

The claims of Hume and Kant—and indeed those of the Logical Positivists and their successors—about the practical, or theoretical, impossibility of such knowledge should also be compared with the long traditions of negative theology. These maintain that the nature of God passes so far beyond the comprehension of any creature that He must be characterised largely or entirely by indirection—as Infinite (not finite), as Incomparable (not to be compared with anything), and so on. Thus Aquinas contrives on other occasions to tell us as much as his most practical Church could wish about the deeds, plans, and demands of the Ineffable. Yet he does also have his ostensibly nescient moments. It was he, too, who in a characteristic attempt at compromise elaborated a doctrine of

analogical predication designed to show how it is possible for
finite creatures to say and to understand something positive
about the infinite God. By contrast Moses Maimonides, often
dubbed anachronistically 'the Jewish Aquinas', was much more
drastic than his successor, 'the Christian Maimonides', in his
insistence that everything which can be truly said about the
Creator—not excluding that He exists—has to be construed as
purely negative. What he seems not to have seen is how
dangerous this must be to his religious commitments.

3. Agnosticism and religion
In Section 1(iii) I argued, following Huxley, that we can
without self-contradiction speak of a religious Agnosticism. It is
nevertheless difficult to keep the two horses in joint harness.

   (i) The easiest case is where the religion is altogether lacking
in doctrinal content. Thus Huxley's latest biographer maintains
that the Scottish sage Thomas Carlyle "taught him that a deep
sense of religion was compatible with an entire absence of
theology" (Bibby, p. 59). If and in so far as such "a deep sense
of religion" really does require no propositional beliefs, then
there is no problem at all. There is nothing here to be or to fail
to be Agnostic about.

   (ii) A second case is that where worship is supposedly
directed at some suitable object for worship, but where the
implicit assumption of the existence of such an object is
combined with explicit and total non-commitment about any
distinguishing attributes:

   He is not a male: He is not a female: He is not a neuter
   He is not to be seen: He neither is nor is not
   When He is sought He will take the form in which He is sought
   It is indeed difficult to describe the name of the Lord.[7]

In its original setting, this expression of a Hindu piety has power
and charm. Yet a moment's thought reveals its intellectual
inadequacy. Considered in that aspect, it recalls nothing so
much as Herbert Spencer's comically pretentious hypostatisa-
tion of The Unknowable. For to affirm the existence of a Being
about which absolutely nothing else can be said must be,
surely, indiscernible from affirming no Being at all? Such
wholesale nescience cannot consist with a conviction that the

supposed object of worship is worthy of worship, or even that there actually is any object of worship at all.

Nor should it be allowed to be any great improvement to say that much more can be said—but only in words all of which must here bear a special meaning; unless, of course, those special made-to-measure meanings can be specified. It was, it may be recalled, the suggestion that the alleged goodness of the Christian God might thus be goodness in an entirely peculiar sense which provoked the anger of John Stuart Mill against Dean Henry Mansel's Bampton Lectures on *The Limits of Religious Thought*.

(iii) A third—and perhaps at first sight more promising— avenue for reconciliation essays a distinction between the essence or the internal nature of God and His external relations with His creation. It is then suggested that, while our knowledge of the former must be at best exiguous and at worst simply lacking, we can nevertheless know as much as we need to know about the latter. As to the rest we should be reverently Agnostic.

In more fashionable terms, this suggestion is that God is, as it were, the 'Black Box'; and that, while we can know enough to be going on with about what it does, we cannot know anything about its own internal arrangements. This is a perfectly possible contrast. But if it is to have application, then the analogue of the 'Black Box' has to be something which can be independently identified. It will not do to specify it as simply the putative unknown cause of whatever we have a mind to construe as its effects. We have to know at least something of what it is supposed to be in order to know that a suitable object does in fact exist for us to be reverently Agnostic about.

If we are to speak here consistently and with warrant of a religious Agnosticism, then the religious Agnostic must believe that he does know at least this essential minimum about the object of his religion, and that it is only at some later stage that Agnostic principle requires him "frankly and honestly to recognise the limits of . . . knowledge".

4. *Rejections of the Agnostic Principle*

What cannot by any means be squared with Agnosticism in Huxley's sense are attempts to transmute the very limitations of human knowledge into grounds for accepting some otherwise unwarranted faith. Such attempts appear to be perennially attractive to those with a different understanding of the ethics of belief. They have been and are made in the interests of many mutually irreconcilable ideological systems.

(i) Perhaps the most famous of them all is the argument now known as Pascal's Wager. This had certainly been deployed in defence of Islam before Pascal pressed it into the service of Catholic Christianity. I shall be examining this argument more closely in Chapter Five. It is enough here to notice that it constitutes a direct, reasoned, rejection of the Agnostic Principle; a rejection in which the reason proposed for believing is a motive for self-persuasion, rather than some evidence of truth.

When in 'The Will to Believe' William James develops the best-known systematic attack on that principle it is, rightly, Pascal whom he hails as his first inspiration. James distinguishes those hypotheses which, for any individual, represent psychologically "live options" from those which do not. He urges that, where a decision between such "live options" cannot be made on evidential grounds, it is right and proper for our choice to be determined by our passional natures. For sometimes such firm commitments may help to make the belief come true, and often we have to act on one unproved hypothesis or another.

The answers to these two points can be as short as they are decisive. First: it would be grotesque to suggest that the basic beliefs in God, Freedom, and Immortality are such as can be made true by our determinedly thinking so.[8] Second: to act upon an hypothesis with decision and effect it is by no means necessary to hold that hypothesis to be a known truth. I always welcome the chance to quote again words of the hero Stadtholder William the Silent: "It is not necessary to hope in order to act, nor to succeed in order to persevere."

(ii) Deservedly famous though Pascal's Wager is, it is only one of many alchemical attempts to transmute ignorance into knowledge. St Augustine of Hippo, for instance, felt the challenge of Classical Scepticism as he met it in Cicero's dialogues *On the Nature of the Gods* and *The Affairs of the Academy*. He gave his own response *Against the Academicians*. The challenge, he thought, can only be overcome with the help of Divine revelation. At the end of the eleventh century, the Arab Al-Ghazali deployed Sceptical arguments similarly, but this time as a propaedeutic to the acceptance of a rival revelation. With the rediscovery by the West in the sixteenth century of the works of Sextus Empiricus, a course of Classical Scepticism became a standard preliminary to fideist commitment. (Fideism is the thesis that truth in religion is accessible only to faith.) The purpose of the course was to persuade that reason cannot attain truth. Yet certainty in true religious belief was still thought absolutely necessary for salvation. Luther was speaking for his time when he thundered against the extremely cautious and restricted Agnosticism of Erasmus: "The Holy Spirit is no Sceptic!"

The only resort was, it seemed, faith: whether the easy-going Roman Catholicism of Michel de Montaigne; the polemical Counter-Reformation fervour of Gentian Hervet, veteran of the Council of Trent, and Latin translator of Sextus Empiricus; or the vestigial Huguenot loyalty of Pierre Bayle—stocker of that great arsenal of secular enlightenment, Bayle's *Historical and Critical Dictionary.*

All this constitutes a fascinating field for the historian of ideas.[9] But our concern is to appreciate why these particular ideas will not do. Allow that if we are to have any knowledge of God, then this must depend largely or wholly upon any special steps which—if He exists—He may have taken to reveal Himself. Still we must never for one moment forget that, if a commitment of faith is not to be arbitrary and frivolous, then we have got to have some good reason for believing: first, that there is a God who has so revealed Himself; and, second, that our preferred candidate—and not one of its innumerable rivals—truly is that revelation.

These points are crucial: both for the appreciation of the history of ideas; and for a reasonable contemporary understanding. They were, as we might have expected, seized by Aquinas. As we have seen, he described any such unsupportable and unsupported commitment as "frivolous" (Section 4(iii) of Chapter One), and proceeded to give what seemed to him, if not to us, sufficient reasons for accepting Christianity rather than either Judaism or Islam as the authentic revelation. These same minimum requirements of seriousness and rationality were similarly appreciated in other religious traditions. Thus, although that usually excellent work *The Encyclopaedia of*

Philosophy describes Al-Ghazali's Jewish contemporary Yehuda Halevi as "concerned to bring men to a mystical and non-rational appreciation of religious truths", Halevi's main work is entitled *Kuzari: The Book of Proof and Argument in Defence of the Despised Faith*. It does in fact offer evidence for the truth of Judaism.

Classical Scepticism as a propaedeutic to faith in some putative revelation has long since fallen out of fashion. But the same fundamental challenge must be put to every response to Kant's famous invitation, made in the Preface to the Second Edition of his *Critique of Pure Reason*: "I have found it necessary to deny knowledge in order to make room for faith."

Natural theology may be, for Hume's reasons, reinforced by those of Kant himself, impossible. The way of religious discovery may indeed be mystical experience, personal encounter with the Divine Thou, or whatever else. Or it may not; and there may not be any religious reality to discover. But there is, and can be, no substitute for having some sound grounds for identifying your experience not only as really mystical but also as experience of the real God; your faith in your putative revelation not only as real religious faith but also as faith in a genuine revelation of the Real; your supposed discovery as a discovery of what actually is independently the case; and so on.

The decisive objection to any and every rationally unfounded flight into faith was put by Locke, who in his *Essay* set a tone of coolly unfervent Anglicanism for the following century:

> . . . we may as well doubt of our own being, as we can whether any revelation from God be true. So that faith is a settled and sure principle of assent and assurance, and leaves no room for doubt or hesitation. Only we must be sure that it be a Divine revelation, and that we understand it right: else we shall expose ourselves to all the extravagancy of enthusiasm, and all the error of wrong principles . . . (IV (xvi) 14).

CHAPTER 3

'The Religious Hypothesis'

In 1739, at the age of twenty-eight, Hume published the first two books of *A Treatise of Human Nature*, the third following in 1740. But, alas, as he was to sigh in the fragment on 'My Own Life' written in the year of his death: "Never literary attempt was more unfortunate. . . . It fell deadborn from the press, without reaching such distinction as to excite even a murmur among the zealots." In 1748 Hume tried again, publishing his *Philosophical Essays concerning Human Understanding*, which he later re-titled *An Inquiry concerning Human Understanding*: "But this piece was at first little more successful than the *Treatise of Human Nature*." However, a year or so later and after the publication of two further works: "My bookseller A. Millar informed me that my former publications (all but the unfortunate *Treatise*) were beginning to be the subject of conversation, that the sale of them was gradually increasing, and that new editions were demanded. Answers by Reverends and Right Reverends came out two or three in a year. . . ."

This was no exaggeration. For this first *Inquiry* went into a second edition in 1751 and a third in 1756; while two counterblasts were published in 1751, four in 1752, five in 1753, three in 1754, and two in 1755.[10] What drew most of the fire was Section X, 'Of Miracles'. In it Hume's aim was to show, from the very nature of the concept of the miraculous, that there must be a peculiar and extraordinary difficulty in establishing that a miracle has occurred; and that for this reason, reinforced by others mainly of a less fundamental kind, "a miracle can never be proved, so as to be the foundation of a system of religion" (pp. 137 and 127).

But this section, as we have already had occasion to notice in Section 2(i) of Chapter Two, is one of a pair. The aim of the other, Section XI, is to undermine what Hume considers to be both the most powerful and the most popular of all the arguments of natural theology. (Natural theology is the attempt to establish the existence of a God with at least a basic minimum of essential attributes, by reference only to general facts about man and nature, and without any appeal to any supposed special revelation from that God.)

The argument which Hume deemed most worthy of consideration is usually known as the Argument from Design. I prefer to call it the Argument *to* Design. For at its best and strongest it does not move, from the disputatious and question-begging premise that the Universe is an artefact, to the necessary conclusion that it must have been made by an Universe-Maker. Instead it proceeds, from the undisputatious and unprejudicial premise that the Universe manifests the regularities and the integration which it does manifest, to the conclusion that these phenomena, and indeed the very existence of the Universe, can only and must be explained by the postulation of a Designer and Maker of all things.

1. Removing the wrappings

The reason why Section X drew so much more fire than Section XI is that Hume was in the former as provocative as in the latter he is circumspect. His treatment 'Of Miracles' begins with a transparently ironic tribute to the late Latitudinarian Archbishop Tillotson, and ends with two of the most mordantly derisive sentences which even Hume ever wrote. But the other is cautiously represented as the gist of a "conversation with a friend who loves sceptical paradoxes; where, though he advanced many principles of which I can by no means approve, yet, as they seem to be curious and to bear some relation to the chain of reasoning carried on throughout this *Inquiry*, I shall here copy them from my memory as accurately as I can in order to submit them to the judgement of the reader" (pp. 142 and 132).

In this caution Hume was wise after his own generation. For, whereas in the first of these two sections he was attacking openly and directly in an area where Deist writers had been sniping for a long time, in the second he was sapping to undermine a formerly unchallenged citadel.[11] Thus Butler's *Analogy of*

Religion, the classic contemporary reply to the Deists, simply assumed that the Argument to Design was unthreatened and undisputed common ground: "There is no need of abstruse reasonings and distinctions, to convince an unprejudiced understanding, that there is a God who made and governs the world, and will judge it in righteousness . . . to an unprejudiced mind ten thousand thousand instances of design cannot but prove a designer" (II (ix)).

(i) We should not be surprised, therefore, to find Hume wrapping up his subversive suggestions so carefully that most of his readers failed, and still fail, to appreciate their full and revolutionary significance. So let us try to bring this shy argument out into the open naked. The first veil is the section title on which Hume eventually settled. Any reader expecting a discussion 'Of a Particular Providence and of a Future State' will be disappointed. Hume's own first choice, 'Of the Practical Consequences of Natural Theology', would have been better. For at least part of what he has to say is that it must be impossible in principle to derive from any well-founded natural theology practically relevant conclusions which could not be drawn from direct study of nature itself. The most suitable title would have been his own piquantly provocative phrase "the religious hypothesis". For the main burden of the section is that the whole business of postulating a God as an explanation of the existence and regularities of the Universe is, as a matter of method, radically unsound.

(ii) The second veil consists in the disarming device of representing the bulk of the material as the reported speculations of "a friend who loves sceptical paradoxes". It is, surely, significant that Hume nowhere specifies which are the "many principles, of which I can by no means approve", nor ventures any grounds for this remarkably non-committal alleged dissent.

(iii) The third veil is the Augustan convention of developing the argument in pseudo-Classical terms. The fictitious conversation "began with my admiring the singular good fortune of philosophy, which . . . received its first birth in an age and country of freedom and toleration, and which was never cramped, even in its most extravagant principles, by any creeds, confessions, or penal statutes" (pp. 142 and 132). It proceeds to a speech such as Epicurus might have made before the Athenian people, in defence of the proposition "that, when, in my philosophical disquisitions, I deny a providence and a future state, I undermine not the foundations of society, but advance principles which they themselves . . . if they argue consistently, must allow to be solid and satisfactory" (pp. 145 and 135).

This is a convention congenial both to the age and to Hume personally. Its first advantage for Hume is that it makes his attack more oblique: 'Jupiter' is less directly challenging than 'Jehovah'. Then it enables him to put into the mouth of "a friend" certain ideas about the origin of "speculative dogmas of religion"—by superstition out of philosophy—which he was in 1757 to publish in *The Natural History of Religion*. He is also by the same means able elegantly to introduce a plea for the toleration of such "philosophical disquisitions". Finally, he can thanks to this allow himself some mischievously ambiguous references to "the established superstition", and the like (pp. 143 and 133). We may here recall, parenthetically, that the earliest Christians were by the contemporary establishment described as atheists: the actual doctrinal content of the positive atheism of Chapter One is necessarily determined by the particular context.

2. Hume's preliminaries

'Epicurus' begins by defining "the religious hypothesis", thus marking out the precise nature and limits of the discussion:

> You then, who are my accusers, have acknowledged, that the chief or sole argument for a divine existence (which I never questioned) is derived from the order of nature; where there appear such marks of intelligence and design, that you think it extravagant to assign for its cause, either chance, or the blind and unguided force of matter. You allow, that this is an argument drawn from effects to causes. From the order of the work, you infer, that there must have been project and forethought in the workman. If you cannot make out this point, you allow that your conclusion fails; and you pretend not to establish the conclusion with a greater latitude than the phenomena of nature will justify (pp. 145 and 135–136).

(i) The first move in response is to draw attention to a

necessary consequence of the restriction specified in that last clause:

> If the cause be known only by the effect, we never ought to ascribe to it any qualities, beyond what are precisely requisite to produce the effect: Nor can we by any rules of just reasoning, return back from the cause, and infer other effects from it, beyond those by which alone it is known to us. . . . Allowing, therefore, the gods to be the authors of the existence or order of the universe; it follows that they possess that precise degree of power, intelligence, and benevolence, which appears in their workmanship; but nothing farther can ever be proved, except as we call in the assistance of exaggeration and flattery to supply the defects of argument and reasoning (pp. 146, and 136 and 137).

It will not do, notwithstanding that it is all too often done: first to postulate—in order to account for the existence of the Universe and the order and integration which we have found therein—an intelligent Super power; and then forthwith—without any further reason given—to insist that that hypothetical Being must be, not just sufficiently powerful and sufficiently intelligent to produce the supposed creation, but in sober truth both strictly omnipotent and strictly omniscient. In fact—as has by now been remarked often—evidences of design could not of their very nature point to so extreme a conclusion. For design is essentially a matter of finding within whatever are the given limitations the best available means to whatever are the proposed ends, of exploiting the various strengths and weaknesses of inherently recalcitrant materials, and so on. But a Being which really is both omnipotent and omniscient cannot by definition be subject to any limitations; unless, of course, that Being has itself chosen to become so subject. An appeal to such a choice could render a design hypothesis consistent with the attribution of that design to such a Being. But evidences of design can by themselves point only to a different God, and a much smaller one than the God of mainstream traditional theism.

Things are, if anything, worse with such evaluative characteristics as benevolence or perfection. For here the case is, not that the evidence is insufficient to warrant, but that it appears actually to refute, the desired drastic conclusion. It is relevant to repeat the first of the two basic objections formulated by

Aquinas to any natural theology: "... if of two contrary things one were to exist without limit the other would be totally eliminated. But what is meant by this word 'God' is something good without limit. So if God were to have existed no evil would have been encountered. But evil is encountered in the world. Therefore, God does not exist" (quoted, in Section 5(ii) of Chapter One).

(ii) Hume makes the second move in his own person:

> If you saw, for instance, a half-finished building surrounded with heaps of brick and stone and mortar and all the instruments of masonry, could you not infer from the effect, that it was the work of design and contrivance? And could you not return again, from this inferred cause, to infer new additions to the effect, and conclude, that the building would soon be finished, and receive all the further improvements which art could bestow upon it? If you saw upon the sea-shore the print of one human foot, you would conclude that a man had passed that way, and that he had also left the traces of the other foot. . . . [Defoe had published *Robinson Crusoe* first in 1719—A.F.] Why then do you refuse to admit the same method of reasoning with regard to the order of nature? (pp. 151–152 and 143).

This was indeed the sixty-four guinea question. Hume has allowed, would indeed insist, that experience must be "the only standard of our judgement concerning this, and all other questions of fact" (pp. 151 and 142). He has also urged: "The religious hypothesis . . . must be considered only as a particular method of accounting for the . . . phenomena of the Universe . . ." (pp. 148 and 139). Surely it could be as legitimate to frame some hypothesis about a god, and to attempt with its aid to explain and predict further phenomena, as it is to postulate the existence of atoms, and to try to explain and predict in terms of "the attributes which you so fondly ascribe" to these invisible entities?

(iii) Before proceeding to Hume's answer to the sixty-four guinea question, we must notice that and why this question did not occur to Hume quite as I have reformulated it in the final sentence of the previous paragraph. We have always to remember that Hume wrote under the enormous shadow of "the incomparable Mr. Newton", and that he is throughout following most faithfully the 'Rules of Reasoning in Philosophy' given in Newton's *Principia*; notwithstanding that Newton himself—that 'great unitarian of Trinity'—would certainly not have welcomed this present employment of his rules.[12] Hume therefore, in this one respect at least, resembles Aquinas. Both are guided, and perhaps sometimes misguided, by the best scientific thought then available. (Compare Section 5(i) of Chapter One.)

Newton had ruled, for instance: "We are to admit no more causes of natural things than such as are both true and sufficient to explain their appearances" (Newton, p. 398). So Hume insisted: "When we infer any particular cause from an effect, we must proportion the one to the other, and can never be allowed to ascribe to the cause any qualities, but what are exactly sufficient to produce the effect" (pp. 145 and 136).

Again, for Newton, and hence for Hume too, 'hypothesis' could be a bad word. Thus Newton also rules:

> Whatever is not deduced from the phenomena is to be called an hypothesis; and hypotheses, whether metaphysical or physical, whether of occult qualities or mechanical, have no place in experimental philosophy. In this philosophy particular propositions are inferred from the phenomena, and afterwards made general by induction. Thus it was that the impenetrability, the mobility, and the impulsive force of bodies, and the laws of motion and of gravitation were discovered (Newton, p. 547).

So Hume too insists:

> So far as the traces of any attributes, at present appear, so far we may conclude these attributes to exist. The supposition of further attributes is mere hypothesis; much more the supposition that, in distant regions of space or periods of time, there has been, or will be, a more magnificent display of these attributes, and a scheme of administration more suitable to such imaginary virtues (pp. 146 and 137).

When Hume speaks of "the religious hypothesis", therefore, this phrase for his contemporaries did not have only the piquancy which it still possesses for the modern reader. Religious propositions are, after all, normally put forward: not as corrigible suggestions for further investigation; but as categorically certain truths demanding total personal commitment. The same phrase in Hume also carries important allusive overtones of offence. The suggestion is of arbitrary, gratuitous, and unwarranted speculation. These have since disappeared so completely that it is now possible for apologists to defend their own religious commitments, however ineptly, as being on all fours with the working hypotheses of science.

Important issues are involved here, both about proper methods for scientific inquiry, and about the proper rationale of scientific procedures. Against Newton, and Hume, it must be said that no explanation of why phenomena are as they are can be, strictly speaking, deduced from any theoretically unloaded description of those phenomena. Whatever follows necessarily from such a description will be a restatement of part of, or all, that description itself. So it cannot, as a theoretical explanation must, 'tell us more'. For Newton, and Hume, it has to be said that whatever "bold conjectures" may be offered by theoreticians can be contributions to science only and precisely in so far as they are subject to the disciplines of falsifiability and to the test of their success in leading to new discoveries. In both cases it is essential that such conjectures carry determinate consequences which are themselves logically contingent.

3. Two "killing blows"

We can and must on this occasion bypass the important issues aforesaid.[13] For Hume's answer to his sixty-four guinea question is also, fortunately, an answer to my own post-Newtonian reformulation of that question. The crux, Hume argues, lies in

> The infinite difference of the subjects. . . . In works of human art and contrivance, it is allowable to advance from the effect to the cause, and returning back from the cause, to form new inferences concerning the effect. . . . The case is not the same with our reasonings from the works of nature (pp. 152 and 153; and 143 and 144).

(i) In the first place:

> The Deity is known to us only by his productions, and is a single being in the universe, not comprehended under any species or genus, from whose experienced attributes or qualities, we can, by analogy, infer any attribute or quality in him. . . . The great

source of our mistake in this subject . . . is that we tacitly consider ourselves as in the place of the Supreme Being. . . . But besides that the ordinary course of nature may convince us, that almost everything is regulated by principles and maxims very different from ours . . . it must evidently appear contrary to all rules of analogy to reason from the intentions and projects of men, to those of a Being so different, and so much superior (pp. 153 and 154; and 144, 145 and 146).

The first crucial difference, disrupting the putative parity of reasoning, is that the hypothetical entity in "the religious hypothesis" is one from whose postulated existence no determinate logical consequences could validly be derived. Hume's first response is thus as elegant as it is decisive. He is simply drawing out—with the simplicity of genius—a necessary but unnoticed consequence of the accepted defining characteristics of the theist God. Had not Butler himself argued in the *Analogy*: "Upon supposition that God exercises a moral government over the world, the analogy of this natural government suggests and makes it credible that this moral government must be a scheme quite beyond our comprehension; and this affords a general answer to all objections against the justice and goodness of it" (I (vii)).

It helps to compare and contrast the entirely different case of a straightforwardly finite and anthropomorphic god, conjured up in an attempt to account for some but not all the phenomena of the Universe. Let us postulate, for instance, a sea-god Poseidon, with the familiar attributes of arbitrary human despots; deduce that he will protect his votaries and afflict those who defy him; and then organise some experiments to test our hypothesis. Members of the experimental group are asked to make vows to Poseidon, promising to erect grateful commemorative tablets and other votive offerings if they are returned home safely from their voyages; while the members of the control group are required to express incredulity about the existence of Poseidon, or otherwise to blaspheme against Poseidon's name. Certainly we have here a religious hypothesis of a sort, and certainly it is respectably testable. But of course this is not at all what Hume meant by "the religious hypothesis"; nor yet what his opponents, the theist natural theologians, are supposed to have in mind. There is a world of difference between any such hypothetical god and God.

(ii) In the second place Hume adds, almost as an after-thought, and in his own person, a still more radical obser-vation:

> . . . there occurs to me . . . a difficulty, which I shall just propose to you without insisting upon it. . . . It is only when two species of objects are found to be constantly conjoined, that we can infer the one from the other. . . . If experience and observation and analogy be, indeed, the only guides which we can reasonably follow in inferences of this nature; both the effect and cause must bear a similarity . . . to other effects and causes, which we know, and which we have found, in many instances, to be conjoined with each other. I leave it to your own reflection to pursue the consequences of this principle. I shall just observe, that, . . . the antagonists of Epicurus always suppose the Universe, an effect quite singular and unparalleled, to be a proof of a Deity, a cause no less singular and unparalleled . . . (pp. 156–157 and 148).

This Parthian shot shows that Hume also recognised a second crucial difference, disrupting the putative parity of reasoning. Not only is the hypothetical cause unique, by definition; but the supposed effect is also unique, again by definition. For, although there is a regrettable sense in which the Andromeda Nebula might be spoken of as 'an island universe', the Universe whose existence and regularities "the religious hypothesis" might be thought to explain is specified as including everything there is (with the exception of its possible Creator). But this second essential uniqueness also carries its own devastating consequence. However far back we may be able to trace the—so to speak—internal history of the Universe, there can be no question of arguing that this or that external origin is either probable or improbable. We do not have, and we necessarily could not have, experience of other Universes to tell us that Universes, or Universes with these particular features, are the work of Gods, or of Gods of this or that particu-lar sort. To improve slightly on a famous remark by C. S. Peirce: 'Universes, unlike universes, are not as plentiful as blackberries.'

It may help here to imagine some more than Methusaleh in a space ship approaching some still unexplored 'island universe'.

He might well, to the exasperated distress of his younger colleagues, refer to the wealth of his experience: 'Mark my words. Man and boy these million million years I have . . .'; and so on, and no doubt on and on and on. But the unique Universe is and must be itself all we have. How it is, is just how it is; and that's that.

4. The Stratonician atheism

The conclusion, which I believe that Hume eventually drew, is that we must take the Universe itself and its most fundamental laws as themselves ultimate.[14] This is a version of the Stratonician atheism, emancipated from any Aristotelian hang-ups. To appreciate the strength of such a position, we need to be seized of the point that every system of explanation must include at least some fundamentals which are not themselves explained. However far you rise in an hierarchy of explanations—particular events in terms of general laws, laws in terms of theories, theories in terms of wider and more comprehensive theories, and maybe even further—still there has to be at every stage, including the last stage, some element or some elements in terms of which whatever is explained at that stage is explained. Nor is this inevitability of logic escaped by the theist. For whatever else he may think to explain by reference to the existence and nature of his God, he cannot thereby avoid taking that existence and that nature as itself ultimate and beyond explanation.

This necessity is common to all systems. It is no fault in any, and certainly not a competitive weakness. The Principle of Sufficient Reason—that there has to be a sufficient reason for anything and everything being as it is, was, and will be—is not, as has often been thought, necessarily true. It is instead demonstrably false.[15] Granted this insight, how can we fail to see that there is no possible explanatory point in hypothesising a Cause to which all and only those powers and inclinations necessary and sufficient to guarantee the production of the Universe as it is, are then gratuitously attributed? In what are always said to be the words of William of Ockham: 'Entities are not to be multiplied beyond necessity'.[16]

CHAPTER 4

What are Cosmological Arguments?

Present usage of the expression 'The Cosmological Argument' is most unsatisfactory. There is, apparently, no consensus about either its connotation or its denotation. People do not agree, that is to say, what it ought to mean nor to what it should be employed to refer. Worse still, those who employ the phrase rarely appear to be aware of the extent of this confusion. The tasks I set myself in the present chapter are, first, to indicate what the situation is and, second, to propose for the future a better usage. The extreme modesty of these ambitions may perhaps be agreeably excused with a well-worn quotation from 'The Epistle to the Reader' in Locke's *Essay*: "It is ambition enough to be . . . an underlabourer . . . clearing the ground a little, and removing some of the rubbish that lies in the way to knowledge . . . uncouth, affected, or unintelligible terms. . . ."

1. The present confusion

My illustrations come from the sort of writers, and the kind of contexts, where we might reasonably expect—in both the descriptive and the prescriptive senses of 'expect'—accuracy and clarity.

(i) In *The Encyclopaedia of Philosophy*, edited by Paul Edwards, under the heading 'Cosmological Arguments for the Existence of God', Professor R. W. Hepburn begins by asserting that it is "a name given to a group of interrelated arguments that claim to prove the existence of God from premises asserting some highly general fact about the world, such as that it exists contingently". Hepburn then proceeds to mention what he takes to be two members of this group. First, there is an argument presented by Descartes in the third of his *Meditations*. This proceeds from the premises "that I exist", and that "the conservation of a substance . . . requires the same power and act that would be necessary to create it", to the conclusion that "I know that I am dependent on some Being different from myself". Second, there is Locke's contention in the *Essay*: that, "from the consideration of ourselves . . . our reason leads us to the knowledge . . . that there is an eternal, most powerful and most knowing Being"; because it is, allegedly, "as impossible that things wholly void of knowledge, and operating blindly, and without any perception, should produce a knowing being, as it is impossible that a triangle should make itself three angles bigger than two right angles" (IV (x) 6 and 5).

Of these two specimens, the first may, without too much strain, be regarded as a characteristically self-centred version of an argument proceeding from the "highly general fact about the world", that it consists of substances which "exist contingently". But the second starts from the very much less general fact that this particular universe contains sentient creatures capable of knowledge—creatures such as we are. If this second argument is to be admitted into the cosmological fold, then it becomes hard to see how the Fifth Way of Aquinas is to be kept out. For that begins from a supposed "fact about the world" which is certainly more general than the one seized by Locke. "The Fifth Way", as the *Summa Theologica* has it, "takes off from the directedness of things. For we observe that some things which lack knowledge—natural bodies, for instance—act for the sake of an end" (I Q2 A3). Yet Hepburn obviously wants to follow tradition by distinguishing cosmological from teleological arguments, arguments such as this Fifth Way. Thus he continues immediately: "It does not attempt (as the Ontological Argument does) to derive the existence of God from an analysis of his essential nature alone, nor does it argue from particular manifestations of orderliness or apparent design in the world's structure to a divine designer. It is enough that there is a world—a world of conditioned objects and events."

(ii) Again, in a paper entitled simply 'The Cosmological Argument', and read to the Annual Meeting of the Western Division of the American Philosophical Association in Chicago in May 1971, Professor William L. Rowe opens almost equally broadly: "The Cosmological Argument began with Plato and

Aristotle, flourished in the writings of Aquinas, Duns Scotus, Leibniz, and Samuel Clarke, and was laid to rest by Hume and Kant." Rowe then distinguishes "two high-watermarks in the history", declaring his present determination to concentrate on the second. Of these two the first "is represented by the first three of Aquinas' Five Ways", while the second "is represented by the form the argument takes in the writings of Leibniz and Samuel Clarke". Rowe offers no account here of what he takes to be the connotation of the expression 'The Cosmological Argument'. Nor does he suggest any principle of differentiation between the "two high-watermarks" other than that "the first occurred in the 13th century", whereas the "second occurred in the [17th and the—A.F.] 18th century".[17]

Yet there is a vital intrinsic, and not merely temporal, difference between these two. For Leibniz, and for Clarke, and for all the other philosophical Rationalists, the desired conclusion is that there is a God whose existence is logically necessary, a God whose existence it would be self-contradictory to deny. But for Aquinas in Way Three the crucial conception of necessary being is of a being not naturally liable to decay or dissolution, not naturally subject to development from or to degeneration into something else. In this Thomist sense there are, in his view, many subordinate kinds of necessary beings— angels, human souls, and the heavenly bodies, for three.[18] And it makes sense to say, as he would, that specimens of these kinds are necessary beings—notwithstanding that they must be one and all creatures of the supreme necessary being, God; and hence that they could and would collapse instantly into non-existence if God so decided. What Aquinas is trying to prove is—in terms of the Cartesian argument cited by Hepburn—not a temporally initiating but an ever sustaining First Cause, Prime Mover, and contingently not logically Necessary Being.[19]

The conception which is essential for Leibniz, and which is entirely different from the conception of a necessary being in Aquinas here, is the very same idea—or pseudo-idea—which is crucial to the Ontological Argument. Indeed that scandal to philosophy consists in arguing, from the conceptual legitimacy of precisely such a notion, to the existential conclusion that this most favoured notion must necessarily have application; which, being interpreted, is the conclusion that such a God must necessarily exist.

In order to make things absolutely clear, it may help to quote two key passages from the classics. In Part IV of his *Discourse on the Method* Descartes presents this Ontological Argument:

> I saw clearly that given a triangle then necessarily its three angles must be equal to two right angles. But none of this gave me any reason to believe that any triangle existed in the world. However, on reverting to the examination of the idea I had of a perfect Being I found that existence was comprised in the idea in the way that that of a triangle contains the equality of its three angles to two right angles, or that of a sphere the equidistance of all the points on its surface from the centre—or even more obviously still. And so, consequently, it is at least as certain that God—this perfect Being—is, or exists, as any demonstration of geometry could possibly be.

The second passage comes from Leibniz on 'The Principles of Nature and of Grace founded on Reason'. It presents what is sometimes called the argument *a contingentia mundi* ("from the contingency of the Universe"). Here to say that the Universe is contingent is simply to say that it makes sense to suggest that it might have been different from what it is, or might even not have existed at all. The argument runs:

> Now we must . . . make use of the great principle . . . that 'Nothing happens without sufficient reason'. . . . This principle given, the first question which we have a right to put will be, 'Why is there something rather than nothing?' . . . Next, given that things must exist, it must be possible to provide a reason, 'Why should they exist thus, and not otherwise?' Now this sufficient reason for the existence of the Universe cannot be found in the procession of contingent things. . . . So the sufficient reason, which needs no further reason, must be found outside this procession of contingent things, and is found in a substance which is the cause of that procession and which is a necessary Being containing the reason for His existence in Himself; otherwise we should not have a sufficient reason at which we could stop. And this final reason for things is called God (§§7–8).

Once all this is appreciated, it ceases to seem so clear that Leibniz and Aquinas produced different versions of the same

Cosmological Argument. On the contrary: it looks as if Rowe's two "high-watermarks" have been seen as "high-watermarks in the history" of the same thing only because there is talk of necessary beings in both periods; and as if those who accept this story have not thought to ask whether the meaning of the expressions 'necessary being', and of the corresponding opposite expression 'contingent being', have remained constant.

(iii) We may now challenge the received doctrine that Kant provided the classical refutation of the attempt by Aquinas to develop a valid Cosmological Argument. A very confusing but by no means untypical manifestation of this false doctrine can be found in the Second Edition of Professor John Hick's *Classical and Contemporary Readings in the Philosophy of Religion*. The student who turns up the Topical Index of this currently successful textbook in order to learn about the Cosmological Argument is referred for "Thomas Aquinas' formulation" to a reading including all three Articles of the Question mentioned in Section 1(i). The usual extract from the *Critique of Pure Reason* is then given as "Kant's critique" of the argument there formulated. Hick's Introductory Note tells us: "This name is generally assigned to the Third of Aquinas' Five Ways, the argument from the contingency of the world. . . ."

The more attentive and acute the student, the greater the difficulty in understanding why Kant is so completely confident that the Cosmological Argument presupposes the principle of the Ontological—the notion, that is, not of a contingently but of a logically necessary Being. Such a student is bound to be still more perplexed by the inclusion of the first of these three Articles: which article is often taken to show that Aquinas explicitly rejected the idea which Kant takes as essential in the conclusion of the Cosmological Argument.

The truth—a truth which Hick's misguided students have no means of knowing—is that Kant had no thought of attempting to block the Third Way of Aquinas. He may not even have heard of it. We need to remember that Kant spent all his life in Protestant Königsberg, that the first *Critique* was written nearly a century before the Encyclical *Aeterni Patris* endowed Aquinas with a peculiar vicarious authority, and that Kant's own graduate work was done on Leibniz, and in a climate of Wolffian rationalism.

2. *A modest proposal*

I want to give, or to restore, to the expression 'Cosmological Argument' a connotation as closely consistent as is practically possible with its established denotation; which is, of course, itself neither perfectly determinate nor universally agreed. My proposal is, therefore, deliberately as modest and as conservative as I can make it. This is for the very good reason that such minimum, non-revolutionary proposals are in cases like this much more likely both to be adopted, and to achieve the results intended.

(i) Since it was, surely, Kant who first gave the expression 'The Cosmological Argument' its present currency, even if he did not himself invent it, the attempt to find a satisfactory connotation can most suitably begin from his own magisterial pronouncement. This pronouncement comes in the first *Critique*, in Section 3 of Chapter III of the Transcendental Dialectic:

> There are only three ways of proving the existence of a Deity on the grounds of speculative reason. All the paths leading to this end either begin with determinate experience and the special constitution of the world of sense-experience and rise, in accordance with the laws of causality, from it to the highest cause existing apart from the world; or they begin with a purely indeterminate experience, i.e. some empirical existent; or abstraction is made of all experience and the existence of a supreme cause is inferred from apriori concepts alone. The first is The Physico-theological Argument, the second is The Cosmological Argument, and the third is The Ontological Argument. There are no more, and more there cannot be.

If this classification is to be as comprehensive as Kant intended, then we have to interpret it as a division not into three arguments but into three kinds of argument. Each kind, or type, has various specimens, or tokens. These kinds are distinguished according to their premises by a clear and intelligible principle. If we accept this Kantian principle without amendment, we shall find little difficulty in allocating specimens to their appropriate categories. There will, however, be some surprises in the consequent distribution. Thus all the Five Ways of Aquinas, and not just Way Five only, will have to be rated as examples of Physico-theological Argument.

That these are true consequences of applying Kant's principle of division can scarcely be denied, once we have refreshed our memories of Kant's own words. Some of us have perhaps been too ready to grin at his typically barbarous neologism 'Physico-theological', and hence to mistake that neologism to have been defined as merely a gratuitous synonym for 'teleological'. But Kant's specification of his first category is different, and more comprehensive. He would have us include, not only teleological arguments, but also all those others which take as their premises claims about "determinate experience and the special constitution of the world of sense-experience". So among those others must be included arguments starting from such propositions as, for example: "It is certain as a matter of sense-observation that some things in the world are in motion"; "In the observable world we discover an order of efficient causes, but no case is found, or ever could be found, of something efficiently causing itself"; "Some things we encounter have the possibility of being and of not being, since we find them being generated, and accordingly with the possibility of being and not being"; "Some things are discovered to be more or less good, or true, or noble, than other things, and so on"; as well as "We observe that some things which lack knowledge—natural bodies, for instance act for the sake of an end".

By contrast, what must remain in the second category is any argument for the existence of God which starts, as Kant has it, "with a purely indeterminate experience, i.e. some empirical existent". Thus the author of the article on 'Theism' in *A Concise Encyclopaedia of Philosophy and Philosophers*, edited by J. O. Urmson, was following Kant's usage when he wrote: "The Cosmological Argument takes as its premise that something exists . . ."; and so was Hepburn when he pointed to the question 'Why is there anything at all?" as its prime mover.

(ii) Now, my suggestion is that we should use the expression 'The Cosmological Argument' only to refer to the type which takes as its premise the proposition that there exists a universe, consisting, in Rowe's words, of one or more "beings that could be caused to exist by some other being or could be causes of the existence of other beings". What indeed, could be more cosmological than that? Such a definition remains basically

Kantian. For, although it drops his characteristic reference to experience, it retains his insistence on the "purely indeterminate"; and it is that which permits the continued application of his principle for dividing the Cosmological from the Physicotheological Argument. The positive change is the introduction of reference to a universe. This has the minor and incidental advantage of making the label 'cosmological' obviously apt.

CHAPTER 5

Is Pascal's Wager the Only safe Bet?

The argument known as Pascal's Wager was not in fact invented by Pascal.[20] Yet he was the writer who gave it whatever prominence it has had, and has, within Christendom; and it certainly does sit well with the new fashions in apologetic set by his *Pensées*. Perhaps because the threat to which Pascal appeals is so unspeakably terrible, the argument seems usually either to be accepted, whether explicitly or implicitly, or else ignored, with a smile or a sigh of embarrassment. It is, therefore, worth going back to the original text in order to estimate the validity or invalidity of the argument considered simply as such.

1. The argument stated
The scene is set:

> The immortality of the soul is of such consequence to us, and affects us so deeply, that we would have to be totally devoid of feeling before we could be indifferent as to whether it is true. . . . It requires no lofty mind to understand that in this world there is no true and lasting satisfaction . . . that within a few years death, which threatens us at every hour, will inevitably subject us to the dreadful necessity of everlasting annihilation or everlasting misery. . . . Nothing is so important to a man as his own state, he has nothing to fear so much as eternity; and so it is unnatural that there should be men indifferent to the loss of their being and to the peril of everlasting misery (11: 194).[21]

(i) So what is to be done?: " 'Either God exists, or He does not'. To which view shall we incline? Reason cannot decide for us one way or the other . . ." (343:233). That third statement needs to be emphasised. Whether true or false it is, surely, at least retrospectively heretical? For, as we saw in Section 2(i) of

Chapter One, it is now a defined dogma of Roman Catholicism that "the one and true God our creator and lord can be known for certain through the creation by the natural light of human reason". Pascal is by contrast expressing the fideism described in Section 4(ii) of Chapter Two.

But, whether or not this position is or was heretical, and whether or not Pascal is correctly interpreted as categorically committed to it in his own person, it certainly is the argued assumption from which Pascal's Wager begins: "If there is a God, He is infinitely incomprehensible, since, having neither parts nor limits, He has no affinity with us. We are incapable, therefore, of knowing either what He is or if He is" (343:233). Again: "It is a remarkable fact that none of the canonical writers ever employed nature to prove God. . . . David, Solomon and the rest never said: 'There is no void, therefore there is a God'. They must have had more knowledge than the most learned men who came after them, all of whom have used that argument. This is highly significant" (19:243). And again: "God has willed to hide himself . . . *Vere tu es Deus absconditus* ('Verily thou art a hidden God')" (449:585).

(ii) It is from this total ignorance that the betting situation is supposed to arise: "Reason cannot decide for us one way or the other: we are separated by an infinite gulf. At the extremity of this infinite distance a game is in progress, where either heads or tails may turn up. What will you wager?" (343:233). This is a game in which you cannot avoid taking part. For from the mere fact of being alive the placing of a bet becomes inescapable. Try to refuse and your pretended disengagement amounts in effect to a bet against the existence of God: "A bet must be laid. There is no option: you have joined the game. Which will you choose, then?" (343:233). It would seem that there can be only one sane answer. Bet your life on God: if you win you win an eternity of ecstasy; if you lose you lose the life you spent in the service of an illusion. Bet your life on no God: if you win you have your brief life, and then annihilation; if you lose you suffer tortures without end. "Thus our proposition is of infinite force, when there is the infinite at stake in a game in which there are equal chances of winning and losing, but the infinite to gain. This is conclusive, and if men are capable of truth at all, there it is" (343:233).

2. Peripheral objections

There are some less central points to notice before we reach the heart of the matter.

(i) Pascal himself raises one objection: " 'I am so made that I cannot believe. What then do you wish me to do?' " The reply is that you can cure your unbelief in the way that others have done; by acting as if you believed until in the end you do: "Follow the way by which they set out, acting as if they already believed, taking holy water, having masses said. . . ." (343: 233).

Pascal's observation of the psychology of self-persuasion is no doubt penetrating. Nevertheless there are two points of very different sorts to be made in passing. First, Pascal says: "But understand at least that your inability to believe is the result of your passions; for, although reason inclines you to believe, you cannot do so" (343:233). The word 'reason' is now being employed in a quite different sense. We started from the disjunction, " 'Either God exists, or He does not' ", and with the claim, "Reason cannot decide for us one way or the other". Reason then was a matter of evidence, and to have had good reason to believe would have been to have had evidence sufficient to warrant the conclusion that the proposition 'God exists' is in fact true. But reason has since become a matter not of evidence but of motive.

If now "reason inclines you to believe" when before you were not so inclined, it is because Pascal's argument has persuaded you that it would be madly imprudent not to brainwash yourself into conviction. Nothing has been said—and, of course, Pascal does not for one moment pretend to have said anything—to show that the evidential situation is after all not as it was at the beginning assumed to be. Certainly there is a perfectly respectable sense of 'rational' in which it is true to say that Pascal's Wager is a contribution to rational apologetic. Yet we must never for one moment overlook that the aims and nature of this new model apologetic are radically different from those, for instance, of the Five Ways of Aquinas.

Second, Pascal continues: "What have you to lose? . . . You will be faithful, honest, humble, grateful, generous, a sincere friend, truthful" (343:233). Pascal's presentation of the moral balance-sheet cannot be allowed to pass unaudited. Deliber-

ately to set about persuading yourself of the truth of a conclusion which is not warranted by the available evidence is
flatly to reject the Agnostic Principle. Not for nothing has
Pascal been recognised, as we saw in Section 4(i) of Chapter
Two, to be the great patron of the reasoned rejection of that
principle. And yet, as was also suggested in that chapter, it is a
principle fundamental to personal and intellectual integrity.
Again, due weight must be given to the fact that a Roman
Catholic commitment involves the acceptance of certain
humanly disastrous practical norms; norms which are today
widely repudiated by non-Catholics not just, as is sometimes
suggested, as inconvenient but as wrong.[22]

This last is not a point to do more than mention in a book of
this sort, especially since the questions did not arise in Pascal's
day as they do now. But it is not similarly anachronistic to
suggest another item for the other side of the balance-sheet.
In order to be accepted as holding the full Catholic faith it is not
enough resentfully to believe that the Universe is in fact under
management of such and such a kind: within that system the
devils and the damned presumably satisfy this requirement. It is
necessary also to praise these various arrangements as quintes-
sentially excellent.[23] "There is", as Pascal himself remarks, "a
great difference between the knowledge and the love of God"
(727:280).

But it is part of the very framework of Pascal's Wager that it
is, or would be, part of God's arrangements that anyone who
fails to take the steps required for safety incurs the penalty of
agony eternal. Now, if anything at all can be known to be
wrong, it seems to me to be unshakably certain that it would be
wrong to make any sentient being suffer eternally for any
offence whatever. Thus a religious commitment which must
involve the glorification of such behaviour as if it were a
manifestation of perfect justice and goodness would be
repugnant to ordinary decency and humanity; even if the facts
were such that in prudence we had to trample down our
generous impulses in a rat-race for salvation.[24]

(ii) Pascal is outraged "that there should be men indifferent
to the loss of their being and to the peril of everlasting misery. . . .
This neglect in a matter which concerns themselves, their
eternity, their all, moves me to anger rather than to pity; it

astonishes and frightens me; I regard it as a monstrosity"
(11:194).

To regard such neglect as some kind of monstrosity may be
reasonable enough. But it should not be taken as obvious that
it is a kind of monstrosity deserving punishment, much less
eternal punishment. It is, I suggest, at least as plausible, to put
it no higher, to urge a very different response. Grant that the
issues really are as Pascal makes out. Then the man who failed
to act as recommended would show himself to be madly
improvident, every bit as blind and foolish as he is accused of
being. But, surely, the just conclusion to draw here is that a
creature so demented could not properly be held accountable
at all? The failure to be deterred by a threat so infinitely
terrible could be taken to constitute overwhelmingly good
reason for saying that the balance of the agent's mind must be
disturbed.

Such considerations of ordinary justice and humanity Pascal
himself would have dismissed with knowing contempt.
Certainly he writes about Original Sin:

> ... nothing shocks our reason more than to say that the sin of the
> first man has rendered guilty those who, being so remote from
> that source, seem incapable of participation therein. This flow of
> guilt seems to us not only impossible but also quite unjust. For
> what is more contrary to the rules of our own poor system of
> justice than to damn eternally an infant incapable of willing, for
> a sin . . . committed six thousand years before he came into
> existence? (246: 434).

What indeed? Pascal, before his conversion, felt exactly the
same. But "that is where I erred; for I believed that human
justice was essentially just, and that I was equipped to know and
judge of it" (290: 375). Was that word 'conversion', or
'perversion'?

(iii) To remove the bad taste left by such attempts to justify
the utterly unjustifiable, savour for a moment the coolly
charitable judgement of Hume in the *Treatise*:

> ... let us consider . . . what divines have displayed with such
> eloquence concerning the importance of eternity; and at the same
> time reflect . . . that the strongest figures are infinitely inferior to
> the subject. And after this let us view . . . the prodigious security

B

of men in this particular. I ask, if these people really believe . . .
what they pretend to affirm; and the answer is obviously in the
negative. . . . The Roman Catholics are certainly the most
zealous of any sect in the Christian world; and yet you will find
few among the more sensible people of that communion, who do
not blame . . . the massacre of St. Bartholomew as cruel and
barbarous, though projected and executed against those very
people, whom without any scruple they condemn to eternal and
infinite punishments (I (iii) 9).

3. The heart of the matter

Pascal's Wager is, however, primarily and essentially an appeal
to the prudent calculation of individual self-interest. It is high
time to meet it head on as such. The central and fatal weakness
of this argument as an argument is that Pascal assumes, and has
to assume, that there are only two betting options; notwithstanding that the predicament which requires that a bet be
made is characterised, and has to be characterised, in such a
way as to preclude any such restriction on the range of
possible alternatives. To make the Wager work Pascal has to
assume that there is only one possible Hell-consigner to be
considered. Yet, to get his betting situation, he has to insist that
"Reason cannot decide for us one way or the other"; that this is
an area of total—repeat, total—ignorance.

The two betting choices offered are: God (the God, and the
whole system, of Roman Catholicism); or no God (of any sort,
and no immortality). No doubt for Pascal and for most of his
contemporary compatriots these were the only two options
which were—in the happy phrase of William James—psychologically live options. But this most parochial and subjective
fact constitutes no relevant reason why these should be the only
options recognised here. We are supposed now to be engaged
in a sober and realistic calculation in a cosmic context of our
objective interest. So, in terms of the distinction made in
Section 2(i) between two fundamentally different senses of
'reason', only a reason of the evidencing kind can be
appropriate and to the point.

In thus limiting our betting choices to two, Pascal makes a
gigantic, unwarranted, and false assumption—an assumption
which is also inconsistent, both with the original framework
general claim that this is an area of total ignorance, and with

some of his own more particular and this-worldly statements elsewhere in the *Pensées*. This gigantic, unwarranted, and false assumption is the assumption that there is only one Hell-threatening possibility, to be matched against the annihilation-promising no-God possibility.

Yet, of course, Pascal was on other occasions perfectly well aware, not merely that there are such other theoretical possibilities, but also that several of these theoretical possibilities have been and are widely advocated as being in fact the truth. Thus he elsewhere argues for the truth of Christianity as against that of some of these rivals on the grounds of the alleged fulfilment of its alleged prophecies:

> I see many religions, all of them contradictory and therefore all false, except one. Each invites belief upon its own authority, and threatens unbelievers. I do not, therefore, believe them. Anyone can make such a demand, anyone can call himself a prophet. But I behold Christianity, in which prophecies have been fulfilled; and that is what everyone cannot do (389: 693).

It is perhaps just worth pointing out that Pascal is entitled to infer, from the fact that all of several positions involve the repudiation of all the others, only that not more than one of these several can be true, not that at least one must be. It is rather a bad lapse.

But what we have to recognise, in assessing Pascal's Wager itself, is that there is no limit to the total of theoretically possible, mutually exclusive, Hell-threatening cosmic systems. In particular, for every such system demanding one way of life, and threatening all others, there is a possible system threatening just that way of life, and rewarding all others. For every possible way of life, there are possible systems demanding and penalising that way of life. And so on. Catholicism threatens with endless torture all those outside the true Mystical Body of Christ; but it is just as conceivable that there is a hidden God (*Deus absconditus*!) who will consign all and only Catholics to the fate which they so easily approve for others. Since there is thus an unlimited range of pairs of possible transcendental religious systems, encouraging and threatening every conceivable way of life with exactly the same inordinate rewards and punishments, such transcendentally backed threats cannot provide even a prudential reason to choose one way of life rather than another. Only if some good evidencing reason can be found, either to limit the range of available betting options, and or to show that one of these options is more probable than its rivals, can the original Wager argument, or any amended version, have any force at all.

That very ignorance of the incomprehensibly transcendent to which Pascal appeals to try to generate his betting situation is really the best of reasons for saying that we have no sufficient reason to rule out any of this unlimited range of possible self-consistent yet mutually exclusive systems. "If there is a God, He is infinitely incomprehensible, since . . . He has no affinity with us. We are incapable, therefore, of knowing either what He is or if He is" (343:233). The true implication to be drawn from Pascal's own premises is, therefore, not that we have to make a reasoned bet, but that we cannot make a reasoned bet. For to weigh odds we need to have a finite range of options. But with regard to the transcendent there is no limit to the range. No odds can be given. The whole idea of placing reasoned bets breaks down. No dice; no Wager.

Part II
FREEDOM

CHAPTER 6

'Theology and Falsification': Silver Jubilee Review

The thousand words of my essay 'Theology and Falsification' were written and first published in 1950. They were published in the first issue of a small and short-lived Oxford journal, *University*. Several comments on the same scale followed in that and later issues. In 1955 this paper, two of those responses, and a rejoinder were included in *New Essays in Philosophical Theology*, along with a much more substantial article directly provoked by that controversy (Flew and MacIntyre (Eds.), pp. 96–130). 'Theology and Falsification' has since been reprinted at least eighteen times, mainly in collections of elementary philosophical readings compiled for the enormous North American college textbook market. It has also received some other marks of attention, even notoriety. For instance: a merrily illustrated version of its opening parable appeared, with due acknowledgement, in the programme of the London production of the successful play, *Jumpers*. Again: several key sentences were reprinted, this time without either quotation marks or acknowledgement, as part of an attack on "the myth of organised crime", the idea that "a national syndicate . . . dominates organised crime throughout the country"—in a criminological study with the catchy title *The Honest Politician's Guide to Crime Control* (Hawkins and Morris, pp. 211–212).

All this makes it scarcely possible to omit a treatment of 'Theology and Falsification' from any selection of my papers in this area. Yet when a piece of literary property has entered to this extent into the public domain, I do not think that its author should feel free to make such drastic revisions as I am now persuaded are required. I shall, therefore, in Section

1 reproduce the full text as published in *New Essays in Philosophical Theology*, merely standardising the references; and I shall then add in Section 2 some new and, I hope, improved thoughts.

1. *'Theology and Falsification'*

Let us begin with a parable. It is a parable developed from a tale told by John Wisdom in his haunting and revelatory article 'Gods' (Flew (Ed.) (1), pp. 187–206). Once upon a time two explorers came upon a clearing in the jungle. In the clearing were growing many flowers and many weeds. One explorer says: 'Some gardener must tend this plot.' The other disagrees: 'There is no gardener.' So they pitch their tents and set a watch. No gardener is ever seen. 'But perhaps he is an invisible gardener.' So they set up a barbed-wire fence. They electrify it. They patrol with bloodhounds. (For they remember how H. G. Wells's *The Invisible Man* could be both smelt and touched though he could not be seen.) But no shrieks ever suggest that some intruder has received a shock. No movements of the wire ever betray an invisible climber. The bloodhounds never give cry. Yet still the Believer is not convinced: 'But there is a gardener, invisible, intangible, insensible to electric shocks, a gardener who has no scent and makes no sound, a gardener who comes secretly to look after the garden which he loves.' At last the Sceptic despairs: 'But what remains of your original assertion? Just how does what you call an invisible, intangible, eternally elusive gardener differ from an imaginary gardener or even from no gardener at all?'

In this parable we can see how what starts as an assertion, that something exists or that there is some analogy between certain complexes of phenomena, may be reduced step by step to an altogether different status, to an expression perhaps of a "picture preference" (Wisdom, pp. 10ff.). The Sceptic says there is no gardener. The Believer says there is a gardener (but invisible, etc.). One man talks about sexual behaviour. Another man prefers to talk of Aphrodite (but knows that there is not really a superhuman person additional to, and somehow responsible for, all sexual phenomena).[25] The process of qualification may be checked at any point before the original assertion is completely withdrawn and something of that first assertion will remain (Tautology). Mr Wells's invisible man could not, admittedly, be seen, but in all other respects he was a man like the rest of us. But though the process of qualification may be, and of course usually is, checked in time, it is not always judiciously so halted. Someone may dissipate his assertion completely without noticing that he has done so. A fine brash hypothesis may thus be killed by inches, the death by a thousand qualifications.

And in this, it seems to me, lies the peculiar danger, the endemic evil, of theological utterance. Take such utterances as 'God has a plan', 'God created the world', 'God loves us as a father loves his children'. They look at first sight very much like assertions, vast cosmological assertions. Of course, this is no sure sign that they either are, or are intended to be, assertions. But let us confine ourselves to the cases where those who utter such sentences intend them to express assertions. (Merely remarking parenthetically that those who intend or interpret such utterances as crypto-commands, expressions of wishes, disguised ejaculations, concealed ethics, or as anything else but assertions, are unlikely to succeed in making them either properly orthodox or practically effective.)

Now to assert that such and such is the case is necessarily equivalent to denying that such and such is not the case. Suppose then that we are in doubt about what someone who gives vent to an utterance is asserting, or suppose that, more radically, we are sceptical about whether he is really asserting anything at all, one way of trying to understand (or perhaps it will be to expose) his utterance is to attempt to find what he would regard as counting against, or as being incompatible with, its truth. For if the utterance is indeed an assertion, it will necessarily be equivalent to a denial of the negation of that assertion. And anything which would count against the assertion, or which would induce the speaker to withdraw it and to admit that it had been mistaken, must be part of (or the whole of) the meaning of the negation of that assertion. And to know the meaning of the negation of an assertion, is as near as makes no matter. to know the meaning of that assertion. And if there is nothing which a putative assertion denies then there is nothing which it asserts either: and so it is not really an assertion. When the Sceptic in the parable asked the Believer,

'Just how does what you call an invisible, intangible, eternally elusive gardener differ from an imaginary gardener or even from no gardener at all?', he was suggesting that the Believer's earlier statement had been so eroded by qualification that it was no longer an assertion at all.

Now it often seems to people who are not religious as if there was no conceivable event or series of events the occurrence of which would be admitted by sophisticated religious people to be a sufficient reason for conceding 'There wasn't a God after all' or 'God does not really love us then'. Someone tells us that God loves us as a father loves his children. We are reassured. But then we see a child dying of inoperable cancer of the throat. His earthly father is driven frantic in his efforts to help, but his Heavenly Father reveals no obvious sign of concern. Some qualification is made—God's love is 'not a merely human love' or it is 'an inscrutable love', perhaps—and we realise that such sufferings are quite compatible with the truth of the assertion that 'God loves us as a father (but, of course, . . .)'. We are reassured again. But then perhaps we ask: what is this assurance of God's (appropriately qualified) love worth, what is this apparent guarantee really a guarantee against? Just what would have to happen not merely (morally and wrongly) to tempt but also (logically and rightly) to entitle us to say 'God does not love us' or even 'God does not exist'? I therefore put to the succeeding symposiasts the simple central question: 'What would have to occur or to have occurred to constitute for you a disproof of the love of, or of the existence of, God?'

2. Second and subsequent thoughts

The first fault in my conduct of the case leading up to that concluding challenge was pointed out in the original discussion by Professor Basil Mitchell. In my rejoinder I at once acknowledged this fault. I cannot better the statement which I made then.

(i) "Some theological utterances seem, and are intended, to provide explanations or express assertions. Now an assertion, to be an assertion at all, must claim that things stand thus and thus; and not otherwise. Similarly an explanation, to be an explanation at all, must explain why this particular thing occurs; and not something else. . . . Mitchell's response to this challenge is admirably direct, straightforward, and understanding. He agrees 'that theological utterances must be assertions'. He agrees that if they are to be assertions, there must be something that would count against their truth. He agrees, too, that believers are in constant danger of transforming their would-be assertions into 'vacuous formulae'. But he takes me to task for an oddity on my 'conduct of the theologian's case. The theologian surely would not deny that the fact of pain counts against the assertion that God loves men. This very incompatibility generates the most intractable of theological problems the problem of evil'. I think he is right."

My one, rather big, reservation was that the theist "has given God attributes which rule out all possible saving explanations. . . . We cannot say that He would like to help but cannot: God is omnipotent. We cannot say that He would help if only He knew: God is omniscient. We cannot say that He is not responsible for the wickedness of others: God creates those others. Indeed an omnipotent, omniscient God must be an accessory before (and during) the fact to every human misdeed; as well as being responsible for every non-moral defect in the Universe. So, though I entirely concede that Mitchell was absolutely right to insist against me that the theologian's first move is to look for an explanation, I still think that in the end, if relentlessly pursued, he will have to resort to the avoiding action of qualification" (Flew and MacIntyre (Eds.), pp. 106–107 and p. 107).

The penultimate and prepenultimate sentences of the previous paragraph refer to The Free Will Defence, which we shall be examining in Chapter Seven. That this is the theist's classical response to the challenge of his Problem of Evil provides the main though slightly devious reason for including the present Chapter Six in Part Two rather than in Part One. A nicely appropriate, but in itself rather nasty, illustration of the "avoiding action" of the final sentence came up in Section 2(ii) of Chapter Five. Pascal, it will be remembered, after his conversion discovered that God's justice is radically different from what we should uninstructedly have called justice; that God's justice is consistent with, is indeed manifested in, dealings which are by ordinary standards paradigmatically unjust: "Some qualification is made—God's love is 'not a merely

human love' or it is 'an inscrutable love'. . . . But then perhaps
we ask: what is this assurance of God's (appropriately
qualified) love worth, what is this apparent guarantee really a
guarantee against?"

(ii) A second fault in my conduct of the case leading up to
that concluding challenge was "the identification of the 'counts
against' and the 'is incompatible with' relations" (Heimbeck,
p. 123). To say that some occurrence counts against the truth
of a given utterance is not at all the same as saying that that
occurrence is incompatible with its truth. To say the former is
to suggest that the occurrence is evidence against the truth of
the proposition in question. But, of course, it can happen that
all the evidence available points one way while the truth lies
after all in the opposite direction.

I was, therefore, wrong to collapse the distinction between
"the 'counts against' and the 'is incompatible with' relations".
My main argument bore directly only on the latter: "To know
the meaning of the negation of an assertion is . . . to know the
meaning of that assertion. And if there is nothing which a
putative assertion denies then there is nothing which it asserts
either; and so it is not really an assertion." To deal satisfactorily
with the former, the case of counting against, is another and
somewhat trickier matter. It was to this case that among my
earlier critics Mitchell in fact addressed himself. For in the
present terms his point was that the traditional theist
Problem of Evil is a problem for him only and precisely
because he does accept that the occurrence of the evils in
question does count against—is, that is to say, evidence against
(although, he hopes, not decisive evidence against)—what he
wants to assert about his God. That, and only that, is why he
seeks for some explanation which will enable him to avoid the
two other alternatives: either the heavy qualification, or the
total abandonment, of his original position.

Elsewhere I have argued that my failure to make the counts
against/is incompatible with distinction misled other critics in
quite interesting ways.[26] But here I want only to insist that,
though serious enough in itself, this second fault still does not
remove the force of the concluding challenge, which is one
instance of a move which we may label the Falsification
Challenge. For it remains true that no "religious hypothesis"

can have any explanatory or predictive or retrodictive power unless it carries some consequences about what has occurred, or is occurring, or will occur. Generally, and hence in the present particular and especially important case, if you are going to say something which is both relevant and substantial, then you have to pay the corresponding price. Since "to assert that such and such is the case is necessarily equivalent to denying that such and such is not the case", the price of asserting exactly so much more has to be denying exactly so much more. Nothing is gained by thinking up the most perfect and complete explanation to show that your hypothesis is entirely compatible with this that and the other evidence against its truth, unless you have provided some other things whose occurrence or non-occurrence really would be incompatible with what you are saying. It is another occasion to quote my favourite Spanish proverb: " 'Take what you like', said God, 'Take it, and pay for it!'."

(iii) The prime merit of 'Theology and Falsification' is, I suggest, that it continues to be at the same time both challenging and open-minded. In this at least it sits well with both 'The Presumption of Atheism' and 'The Principle of Agnosticism'. Anyone adopting that presumption adopts a posture in which he waits to hear what the believer proposes for our belief, and to examine whatever reason the believer offers for holding that his proposition is in fact true. But just as some have confused a procedural presumption with the prejudicial assumption of a substantive conclusion, so many have misinterpreted a challenge which is in principle open-minded as the rhetorical expression of a comprehensive doctrine about all religious belief or all religious language.

This is a misinterpretation. No appeal is made to a general doctrine about meaning. The nearest approach to any such general doctrine is the appeal to a scarcely contestable necessary truth about assertion: "To assert that such and such is the case is necessarily equivalent to denying that such and such is not the case." Nothing is said about all religious belief or all religious language. The nearest approach to such a general theory seems to be the statement, and the comment: "A fine brash hypothesis may thus be killed by inches, the death by a thousand qualifications. And in this, it seems to me, lies the

peculiar danger, the endemic evil, of theological utterance."
But to say that something may happen is not to say that it
always does, or that it must. And to say that something is a
peculiar danger is not to say that you always do or always must
succumb: a danger to which we cannot but succumb is not just
a danger but an ineluctable fate.[27]

If this were merely a matter of some people thinking that
twenty-five years ago I said something which as a matter of fact
I did not say, then almost nothing could now be less
important. What does remain important is to realise that
religious belief is not in this respect all of one kind; that
different believers—including believers who think of themselves, and are thought of, as believers in the same religion—
will respond to the present challenge in different kinds of ways;
and that sometimes the same person will respond in different
ways on different occasions, even at different moments of the
same discussion. The prime purpose of the challenge is to
reveal—summoning another happy phrase from William
James—"the cash value" of what is apparently or actually
being asserted by one particular believer at one particular
time. But if we proceed to put the challenge on different
occasions, and to different people; then we are also bound to
discover something of that diversity which 'Theology and
Falsification' has sometimes so misguidedly been thought to
deny.[28]

(iv) Certainly I cannot repeat about this piece Hume's
lament for the *Treatise*; which, it will be remembered, "fell
deadborn from the press, without reaching such distinction as
to excite even a murmur among the zealots". So it is perhaps
just a little remarkable that no one seems to have taken up
"One final suggestion" from my first rejoinder:

> The philosophers of religion might well draw upon George
> Orwell's last appalling nightmare *Nineteen Eighty-four* for the
> concept of doublethink. '*Doublethink* means the power of holding
> two contradictory beliefs simultaneously, and accepting both of
> them. The party intellectual knows that he is playing tricks with
> reality, but by the exercise of doublethink he also satisfies himself
> that reality is not violated' (Orwell (2), II (ix): italics original).
> . . . But of this more another time perhaps.

Here and now one part of that more is to notice that the same or similar forms of words may, especially when ideology is involved, be correctly interpreted in one kind of way on one occasion and in another on another. Utterances which in a sophisticated context, and under strong critical pressure, are interpreted as making few if any falsifiable claims, may at other times, and in less exposed circumstances, be construed as affording wide-ranging and substantial guarantees about what will or will not happen. A similar though not exactly the same point is made nicely by Professor P. F. Strawson about certain equivocal utterances in a much less emotionally charged universe of discourse: "Under pressure they may tend to tautology; and, when the pressure is removed, assume an expansively synthetic air" (Strawson, p. 252).

The reference to doublethink is a reminder of the need in this kind of case to attend to—so to speak—the dynamics as well as the statics of belief. For under such strong conflicting pressures as can be involved in these issues of ideology people can, and perhaps typically do, oscillate between two incompatible interpretations of the same form of words, or else insist on having it both ways at once. The Falsification Challenge is not a rhetorical question, but an authentic and—I believe—powerful instrument of inquiry for discovering what actually is being said on different occasions.

A second further point to be made now about doublethink is that the original mention probably appeared to be a suggestion that a notion first conceived in a purely secular, political context should be introduced into the philosophy of religion. Yet many of Orwell's readers must from the first have heard echoes from more traditional and other-wordly conversion documents in, for instance, that grisly final paragraph of *Nineteen Eighty-four*:

> He gazed up at the enormous face. Forty years it had taken him to learn what kind of smile was hidden beneath the dark moustache. O cruel, needless misunderstanding! O stubborn, self-willed exile from the loving breast! . . . But it was all right, everything was all right, the struggle was finished. He had won the victory over himself. He loved Big Brother (Orwell (2), III (vi)).

Biographical material becoming available since Orwell's death shows that he was himself fully aware of these analogies between the secular and the religious varieties of certain religious phenomena; and that, whether rightly or wrongly, he felt a comparable revulsion against both. Thus Christopher Hollis, who knew Orwell and had followed his writings since the two of them had overlapped in their times at Eton, tells how Orwell complained that the radio version of *Animal Farm* cast " 'a sop to those stinking Catholics' " (Hollis, quoted p. 150).[29] It remains only to add that the scope and usefulness of the Falsification Challenge too extends, and was by me always seen to extend, well beyond the sphere of religious discourse. After all I am, unfortunately, old enough to have argued with real Fascists in the 1930s and early 1940s as well as, then and in all the succeeding decades, with representatives of many of the by now surely more than fifty-seven varieties of Marxist-Leninist totalitarian socialism.

CHAPTER 7

The Free Will Defence

1. What this defence is

Consider the theist's Problem of Evil: 'Either God cannot abolish evil or he will not: if he cannot then he is not all-powerful; if he will not then he is not all-good.'[30] The problem is to show that it can after all be consistent to maintain: both that there is a God; and that this God is omnipotent, omniscient, and perfectly good; and that there is nevertheless much evil in what is supposed to be his creation. This problem is usually presented as one of reconciling the God hypothesis with recalcitrant external facts. But—since claims about the sinfulness of men are integral to all the three great theist systems of Judaism, Christianity, and Islam—it may also be seen as one of overcoming an apparent internal inconsistency within the system itself.

The first move in the Free Will Defence is to insist, as Aquinas put it in the *Summa Theologica*, "that nothing which involves contradiction falls under the omnipotence of God" (I Q25 A4); that is to say, that even God cannot do the logically impossible; or, better, that a self-contradictory expression is not miraculously transformed into good sense by being inserted into a sentence in which the word 'God' is the grammatical subject.

The second move is to contend that the capacity to choose is a logically necessary precondition of the realisation of various high values; that it is no more possible for these values to be realised if creatures are not endowed with this capacity, than it would be possible actually to display fortitude without having any pains or hardships to endure, or actually to forgive without at least believing that you had first been injured. The third move is to maintain that God does in fact endow with this crucial capacity certain of his creatures, in particular humans.

The argument is then developed by urging: that this precious

F

yet dangerous 'gift of free will' necessarily implies, not only the possibility of choosing what is good, but also the possibility of choosing what is bad; that the unfortunate, altogether familiar, fact is that some, perhaps most, of God's creatures usually— although the choice and hence the fault is, of course, always theirs and not his—pick wrong rather than right options; but that, nevertheless, all the evil of and consequent upon all these wrong choices by creatures is in the end more than offset by the actually achieved sum of those higher goods of which the capacity to choose is the logically necessary condition.

The precise phrasing of the final clause of the previous sentence is important. What is essential is the capacity to choose either right or wrong. This does not entail that there should actually be any wrong choices. However, granting that in fact many are and will be made, no doubt some at least of these will be put to use as the (logically necessary) foundations of some such goods as actual exercises of fortitude or of forgiveness; and, if so, these will surely serve in turn as items in that sum of actual alleged higher values to which the Free Will Defender appeals in hopes of offsetting, with plenty to spare, the sum of all actual evils in what is supposed to be the creation of his God.

If this defence is to be extended to cover all the admitted evils, then there will presumably have to be some bold factual postulations to make out that much, which does not appear to be either directly or indirectly consequential upon the wrong choices made by creatures, really is. There are also apparently intractable value difficulties to be overcome before it could be allowed that the balance would come down on the side proposed: what can, it is argued, be got only if this 'gift of free will' is given seems in fact to be being purchased at an unacceptably high price in all manner of most unjustly distributed consequential evils. Neither of these two subsidiary objections will arise if the fundamental position of the whole Free Will Defence cannot be held. This key position is that there is a contradiction in the suggestion that God could create a world in which men are able to do either what is right or what is wrong, but in fact always choose to do what is right.

2. Some essential preliminaries
To meet the Free Will Defence we have to have the right

equipment. Still more important, we have to get rid of certain far too popular misconceptions.

(i) The traditional philosophical problems here are very frequently mischaracterised, not only by philosophically uninstructed laymen, but also by many of those paid to know better. The endemic error is prejudicially so to specify the problem that one of two rival kinds of solution is taken as given: the question is put as that of 'Free Will *or* Determinism?'. Yet if that were indeed what the issue was, then what would remain to be investigated would be: not a philosophical question of "the relations of ideas"; but instead a psychological "matter of fact and real existence" (Hume (2), IV (i)). The logically prior, the truly philosophical question is: 'Free Will and Determinism *or* Free Will or Determinism?'.

In this understanding the traditional philosophical problems of freewill are seen as problems of the logical analysis of, and of the logical relations between, members of two ranges of terms and expressions; focusing upon the big divisive question whether the presuppositions and the implications of the application of members of the one set are or are not compatible with those of the application of members of the other set. On the one hand we have all the notions which are apparently essential to the ascription and repudiation of responsibility: 'He acted of his own freewill', for instance, 'He had no choice', or 'He could have done otherwise'. On the other side we have the ideas embraced in such claims as that everything which happens has a cause, or that everything which happens could—in principle, of course—be subsumed under universal laws of nature.

The big divisive question arises because it looks as if the assumptions and the implications of the two sets of notions, both of which we seem to have the strongest of justifying reasons for employing, are in conflict. What we take to be our everyday knowledge of human beings appears to show that it is often truly said that someone could have done differently than he did. Yet the presuppositions and achievements of deterministic science seem to involve that nothing ever could have been other than it was, is, or will be; and that everything which happens occurs as the necessary and inevitable result of antecedent causes. One kind of answer to the big question is to contend that the two sets of notions are largely, or even completely, compatible. Such contentions are now usefully labelled Compatibility Theses. The opposite response is to urge that, on the contrary, they are incompatible. Contentions of this kind are now called, correspondingly, Incompatibility Theses.

(ii) It is much too rarely noticed that most of those classical philosophers who published in this area were Compatibilists of some stripe. Certainly this is true of Hobbes, of Leibniz, of Locke, of the later Hume, and of John Stuart Mill. We shall see later that, with appropriate alterations, much the same can be said of the classical Christian theologians. To appreciate how this is possible we have to recognize a fundamental distinction between two senses of 'free will'. In the technical, philosophically libertarian sense, 'free will' is so defined that a manifestation of free will is necessarily the manifestation of an uncaused cause; and it is usually, though not always, taken to involve a decision the direction of which must be in principle unpredictable. But this technical sense, which is often mistaken to be the only one there is, is in truth quite different from the ordinary, everyday, untechnical sense. For there the contrast is not between uncaused causes and caused causes, nor between the in principle unpredictable and the in principle predictable, but between what was done or chosen freely and what was done or chosen only under constraint.

If you insist on construing 'free will' always in the first sense, then of course it is immediately obvious that a thesis of universal causal determinism could not in any way be reconciled with the reality of free will. But to do this is grossly prejudicial, arbitrarily begging the philosophical question against the Compatibilist. If what we are talking about is free will (libertarian), then there is indeed no room for any compromise: 'Free Will *and* Determinism'. For you the only issue which then remains is not philosophical but psychological: 'Is there in fact such a phenomenon as free will (libertarian)?'

Once we are seized of the fundamental distinction between free will (libertarian) and free will (unconstrained), but only then, we are in line to formulate our problem without prejudice and as a philosophical problem. The question is whether all genuine choice and all true action logically presupposes libertarian free will. If the answer to this not to be prejudiced philosophical question is, as our Incompatibilist maintains, 'Yes', then whenever an action or choice is either free (unconstrained), or not free (unconstrained), it will provide a manifestation of free will (libertarian). If instead the answer is, as our Compatibilist contends, 'No', then an action or choice may well be free (unconstrained) and yet still provide no evidence of free will (libertarian).

(iii) One point in the previous paragraph needs to be underlined. Actions which are not free (unconstrained) can be none the less true actions. Suppose that, threatened by a man with a gun, the Bank Manager opens the safe and reluctantly hand him the contents. Called to account for the losses involved, the Bank Manager pleads compulsion; and this plea in this case is, very properly, accepted as a complete excuse. Nevertheless, although he was forced to do what he did not want to do, although he thus acted not freely but under compulsion, still he did act. His situation was in this respect entirely different from that of a man who is seized by main force and projected through a shop window. The latter, as a human missile, is a victim not an agent. Reproached by the shopkeeper about the breaking of the window the missile man's reply should be: not that he acted under compulsion, and is therefore to be excused; but that it was not he who broke the window, but the toughs who threw him through it.

To act under compulsion is, therefore, still to act. The same holds, with appropriate alterations, for choice. And whenever it is correct to say that someone acts or chooses it must surely be equally correct to say that, in some fundamental sense, he could have acted or chosen otherwise. The content of this fundamental sense of 'could have done otherwise' is, or should be, the crux of the dispute between Compatibilist and Incompatibilist. Both parties ought to be able to agree that that sense, whatever it is, must be distinguished from another, relatively superficial, interpretation of the same expression.

When our Bank Manager protested that he acted under compulsion he might also have pleaded that he had no choice. But it would be silly to construe this plea—as the French would say if only they spoke English—at the foot of the letter. His point would be: not that he had literally no choice in the matter—as the missile man had literally no choice as to whether or not the window was to be broken; but that the only alternative which he did in fact have—that of being gunned down by the bandit—was not one which he could reasonably be required to choose. That there always is some alternative in cases of acting under compulsion, that the agent always does in some more fundamental sense have a choice, becomes quite clear when we consider even more drastic possibilities.

It is one thing to plead, and to accept, compulsion at the point of a gun as a complete excuse when it is a question of surrendering (only!) money; which the police may anyway be able to recover later. It is rather a different thing to offer, and to accept, the same plea as a complete excuse when it comes to a question of betraying comrades in some organisation of resistance to tyranny; or of assisting the SS at Auschwitz, or the KGB in the Katyn Forest. Generally, it would be scandalous for the acceptability of the plea of compulsion to vary with both the severity of the threat and the seriousness of the offence—as it does—were the offender not in this case always an agent who, as such, in the fundamental sense, could have done otherwise.

But there is no such scandal here. For it is proper to plead, 'I had no choice', in the relatively superficial sense, only where, in the fundamental sense, there was an alternative. When Luther at the Diet of Worms thundered, "Here I stand—I can no other. So help me God," he was not denying, but presupposing, that, in our fundamental sense, he could have done otherwise. It would have been grotesque to report the onset of some general paralysis in words so well calculated to express reverberating defiance! Again, at a very much less admirable if more familiar level, when the agents of *The God-father* "make someone an offer which he cannot refuse", it is always true that, in the fundamental sense, he can; even though, very sensibly, he will not. This case is quite different from that of the errant Mafioso who is without warning gunned down from behind; and who, at that moment, and indeed thereafter, in the most literal sense, has no choice.[31]

3. Two attackers distinguished

The preliminaries over it is now time to engage with the

philosophical enemy. In Chapter VI of his powerful study *God and Other Minds*, Professor Alvin Plantinga presents his case for the Free Will Defence as a reaction to two earlier attempts to overcome it.[32] The key position in this defence is, as was said at the end of Section 1, the contention that there is a contradiction in the suggestion that God could create a world in which men are able to do either what is right or what is wrong, but in fact always choose to do what is right.

(i) Plantinga distinguishes two versions of the challenge to this fundamental. The first is put by what I, but not Plantinga, would call a Compatibilist; the second by an Incompatibilist. Plantinga has no respect at all for the former, and thinks to dispose of it in two very brisk moves. The first of these moves is to confess: "It seems to me altogether paradoxical to say of anyone all of whose actions are causally determined that on some occasions he acts freely. When we say that Jones acts freely on a given occasion, what we say entails, I should think, that either his action on that occasion is not causally determined or else he has previously performed an undetermined action which is a causal ancestor of the one in question" (Plantinga, p. 134).

(ii) The Incompatibilist challenger here thinks in distinctively Leibnizian terms about actualising possible beings. God decided which of various possible beings, including in particular possible human beings, would be favoured with actual existence. Yet this second challenger is entirely un-Leibnizian in his assumption that genuine action and authentic choice must presuppose free will (libertarian). While allowing that Omniscience would be able to foresee the directions of all such actions and choices by all actual and possible beings, he still takes it absolutely for granted that all such actions and choices must either be or otherwise entail uncaused causes. No one would ever guess from reading Plantinga that there might be two importantly and relevantly different senses of 'free will', much less that Leibniz's own great *Theodicy* is clearly and unequivocally Compatibilist.

4. The Incompatibilist offensive
Because the assumptions of Incompatibilism seem perfectly obvious to Plantinga, he gives most of his attention to this as the

"more serious" objection (*ibid.*, p. 136). There are two vital assumptions: one philosophical; and the other factual. The first is that the concept of action presupposes libertarian free will. The second is that we do sometimes—indeed continually—act; and that in this sense.

Now, whether or not both these assumptions are both as obvious and as true as Plantinga and so many others believe, they really ought to be seen as presenting some difficulty, perhaps even an insurmountable difficulty, for the essential theist doctrine of Divine creation. For that doctrine apparently requires that, whether or not the creation had a beginning, all created beings—all creatures, that is—are always utterly dependent upon God as their sustaining cause. God is here the First Cause in a procession which is not temporally sequential.[33] Anyone acquainted with the treatment of this doctrine in Aquinas or Calvin, even in Descartes or Leibniz, must find it almost incredible that Plantinga—in this, of course, like the majority of his contemporary coreligionists—can see no difficulty at all about coupling his belief in the existence of God with his conviction of the reality of libertarian free will. For just how is the idea of God as the sustaining cause of all creation to be reconciled with the insistence that this creation includes uncaused causes?

It is, I suggest, significant that in Plantinga's quoted statement of the second, Incompatibilist objection to the Free Will Defence the verbs describing God's supposed activity are all in the past tense: "If God has made men such that in their free choices they sometimes prefer what is good and sometimes what is evil, why could he not have made men such that they always freely choose the good? . . . God was not . . . faced with a choice between making innocent automata and making beings who, in acting freely, would sometimes go wrong; there was open to him the obviously better possibility of making beings who would act freely but always go right" (*ibid.*, p. 136). It was, it may be recalled, precisely because his talk of God's selecting which of all possible beings to favour with existence suggested once for all operations in the comfortably distant past that Leibniz had to be careful to reject any suggestion that God in his system enjoyed only a "nominal kingdom".[34]

Leibniz, as I have said, was clearly and unequivocally

Compatibilist in his philosophical position. He was also equally straightforward in his denial of the reality of libertarian free will as a psychological phenomenon. So it is on this occasion better to cite from another equally classical philosopher passages which in their combination of luminous clarity and flagrant inconsistency should be enough to show the hopelessness of any Incompatibilist version of the Free Will Defence. Descartes says of his God, in Principle XL of Part One of *The Principles of Philosophy*: "His power is so immense that it would be a crime for us to think ourselves ever capable of doing anything which he had not already preordained."

Descartes nevertheless insists, in Principle XLI, that "we are so conscious of the liberty and indifference which exists in us, that there is nothing that we comprehend more clearly and perfectly". So it appears that he wished first to insist that God's omnipotence can leave no room for the sort of ultimate autonomy postulated by believers in the reality of libertarian free will; but that he then went on immediately to affirm that it is a luminously indisputable deliverance of immediate experience, not only that we do enjoy powers of choice and action, but also that the Incompatibilist is right in his understanding of what these powers presuppose. It was, therefore, not without reason that Descartes warned us in the first of these two paragraphs that "we should soon be involved in great difficulties if we undertook to make his pre-ordinances harmonise with the freedom of our will, and if we tried to comprehend them both at one time"!

5. The Compatibilist offensive

Plantinga would dispose of this challenge, for him the first, in two brisk moves. The first move, as we have seen, simply consists in taking it for granted that free will (unconstrained) can either be simply identified with free will (libertarian), or else at least presupposes the prior occurrence of a manifestation of the latter: "When we say that Jones acts freely . . . either his action on that occasion is not causally determined or else he has previously performed an undetermined action which is a causal ancestor of the one in question."

The second move is to waive the first point in favour of an alternative contention: "But we need not try to resolve that issue, for the free will defender can simply . . . state his case using other locutions. He might now hold, for example, not that God made men free and that a world in which men freely do both good and evil is more valuable than a world in which they unfreely do only what is good; but rather that God made men such that some of their actions are unfettered . . . and that a world in which men perform both good and evil unfettered actions is superior to one in which they perform only good, but fettered, actions." The word 'unfettered' is then stipulatively so defined as to entail what I have been calling libertarian free will (*ibid.*, p. 135).

(i) This will not do. First, it is a mistake thus to dismiss questions about the present meanings of the key terms. Allow, just for the moment, that the Compatibilist is right in his belief that words such as 'action' and 'choice' do not carry any implications of libertarian free will. Then, on this assumption, there can surely be no doubt but that we do often act and that we do frequently make choices. And, furthermore, our beliefs about the importance of choice will be beliefs about the importance of choice in this ordinary established sense of the word 'choice'. Suppose that someone now comes along to tell us that we also possess powers of unfettered choice, in the made to measure sense of 'unfettered' specified in the previous paragraph. Suppose too that he also claims that these powers are enormously more valuable than those others which we already knew, prior to his instruction, that we are indeed so fortunate as to exercise. We shall certainly have to demand that some further reasons be given for accepting both his fresh factual contention and his new valuational claim. Plantinga is, therefore, wrong in holding that the opposition thesis about present meaning "is in an important sense merely verbal, and thus altogether fails to damage the Free Will Defence" (*ibid.*, p. 135).

(ii) Consider next the opposite assumption. Suppose that such words really did carry the implication which Plantinga and other Incompatibilists believe that they do carry. It now becomes very hard to see how anyone could ever be in a position to know either that a choice had been made or that an action had been performed. For, according to the supposition: "We use the word 'free' not simply to characterise a certain class of actions which we could, so to speak, pick out by eye, but rather to say of those actions that no complete causal account can be given of them" (Lucas, p. 12).

I borrow this bold formulation from another very able writer; who, as it happens, shares with Plantinga the complicating and, as I have already suggested, mistaken belief that freedom (libertarian) is, like freedom (unconstrained), to be thought of as a possible characteristic not of all actions as such but of some actions as opposed to others. However, whether the claim is, as here, that freedom (libertarian) is what the word 'free' ordinarily means, or whether it is that freedom (libertarian) is part of the ordinary senses of the words 'choice' and 'action', the difficulty is to show how, on this assumption, we can possibly be justified in holding, as we so frequently and so confidently do, that free choice and free action, or simply choice and action, have in fact occurred. The general and notorious obstacles to proving a negative have in recent years been especially well canvassed with respect to the most relevant particular case of 'Every Event has a Cause' (Flew (Ed.) (2), pp. 96–112). Surely too, that some occurrence is one of which "no complete causal account can be given," is conspicuously not the sort of feature "which we could, so to speak, pick out by eye", in the fashion suggested by Descartes.[35]

The force of this objection is, I suggest, concealed from Plantinga and others by their very conviction that freedom (libertarian) is what the word 'free' ordinarily means. If this suggestion is correct, then it underlines the point that the issue of the truth of that conviction is not quite so trifling as they believe. What we do in fact know we must be able to know. But everyone in his commonsense moments is ready to echo Dr Johnson: "We know our will is free, and there's an end on't."[36] Certainly Johnson was at least half right if the first clause in his utterance is to be construed as an insistence that we do know that we very often, in the fundamental sense, could have done otherwise. But he is not even half right, but rather wholly wrong, if that clause is instead construed as making what I take to be the technical, libertarian claim. My suggestion is in effect, that Plantinga, and many others, having first, by interpreting the key terms in one way, reached one conclusion, and this true; have then, by committing themselves to a different understanding of these terms, come to take for granted as equally beyond dispute what has thereby been transformed into the expression of another proposition, and that false.

(iii) In order to illuminate this crucial, fundamental sense of 'could have done otherwise', consider the difference: between those occasions on which I can truly say only, 'My arm moved, but I did not move it'; and those occasions on which I can truly say, 'I moved my arm'. Call the first kind of movement a motion, and the second kind a moving. We are all perfectly familiar with this difference and with all that goes with it, and there can be absolutely no doubt but that there actually are both motions and movings. I submit that it is in terms of this difference, or this family of differences, that our key notion has to be explained. All movings are actions or parts of actions; all action involves movings or abstentions from moving; while choice too surely has to be understood by reference to actions or the possibilities of actions.

This is not the place to develop this contention. But if it is even approximately on the right lines, then it becomes clear that we can entrench ourselves impregnably against any assault upon our commonsense conviction that people could usually—indeed, if we take the word 'do' strictly, could always—do other than they do do.[37] Anyone not totally paralysed must be capable of a variety of possible movings, and, when active, must be all the time realising some of these possibilities. So suppose someone tells us that psychology, or sociology, or what have you, either presupposes, or has shown, that no one ever can do other than he does. Then we reply that: either our informant has misread his psychology, or sociology, or what have you; or else whichever discipline is in question really has got it wrong and, by this perverse commitment to deny the known facts of human action, is discrediting itself. Given our present interpretation of the terms 'free', 'choice', and 'action'—which interpretation is, it is urged, consistent with their ordinary meanings—the problem here becomes: not, whether the progress of the human sciences can leave any room for human freedom; but, rather, to formulate whatever deterministic presuppositions may be required in such a way as not to conflict with these undeniable facts of action and choice.

(iv) There can, therefore, be no basis for either fearing or hoping that advances in the sciences may have shown or may be about to show that, in the fundamental sense, no one ever could do other than they do. By contrast, and more directly to our present purposes, it may seem that from the same true premise, that in our movings we could always do other than we do do, we could legitimately infer the conclusion that our human condition cannot really be what the classical theist theologians have seen it as being. Yet we cannot. For it is, surely, not inconsistent to say that God is the ultimate sufficient condition not only of all motions but also of all movings.

Consider, for instance, how Aquinas in the *Summa contra Gentiles* draws directly from what I take to be agreed essentials of theism precisely that conclusion which when it came from my pen Plantinga so lightly dismissed as "altogether paradoxical". For Aquinas argues that "just as God not only gave being to things when they first began, but is also—as the conserving cause of being—the cause of their being as long as they last . . .; so he also not only gave things their operative powers when they were first created, but is also always the cause of these in things. Hence, if this divine influence stopped every operation would stop. Every operation, therefore, of anything is traced back to him as its cause" (III, 67).

The relevant and uncomfortable implications of that final statement are spelt out fully in two later chapters:

> God alone can move the will, as an agent, without doing violence to it. . . . Some people . . . not understanding how God can cause a movement of our will in us without prejudicing the freedom of the will, have tried to explain . . . authoritative texts wrongly: that is, they would say that God 'works in us, to wish and to accomplish' means that he causes in us the power of willing, but not in such a way that he makes us will this or that. . . . These people are, of course, opposed quite plainly by authoritative texts of Holy Writ. For it says in *Isaiah* (xxvi, 2), 'Lord, you have worked all our work in us.' Hence we receive from God not only the power of willing but its employment also (III, 88–89).

Luther too holds substantially the same position. But we need to take special note of Luther's insistence that this total divine control abolishes none of the familiar, humanly important differences. With his usual vigour the Reformer writes: ". . . I did not say 'of compulsion' . . . a man without the

Spirit of God does not do evil against his will, under pressure, as though he were taken by the scruff of his neck and dragged into it, like a thief or a footpad being dragged off against his will to punishment; but he does it spontaneously and voluntarily" (Luther, II, 8). Where Luther and Aquinas do differ is that Luther still speaks, aggressively, of *The Bondage of the Will*; whereas Aquinas puts forward the characteristically eirenic suggestion that the partial libertarian Origen had misunderstood what is the true Catholic doctrine of the freedom of the will.

(v) Confronted by this much too uncomfortably clear and vivid picture of the relations which would surely have to obtain between men and the God of theism, we may well shudder. Surely, we are inclined to protest, such creatures would be puppets or automata, and it would be utterly monstrous for their Creator to punish them for the faults which he ensures that they have. Monstrous indeed it would be. Just as Pascal very nearly said exactly this of the arrangements described in the doctrine of original sin, so Luther himself very nearly says the same here: "The highest degree of faith is to believe He is just, though of His own will he makes us . . . proper subjects for damnation, and seems (in the words of Erasmus) 'to delight in the torments of poor wretches and to be a fitter object for hate than for love'. If I could by any means understand how this same God . . . can yet be merciful and just, there would be no need for faith" (*ibid.*, II, 7). Later Luther asks: "Why then does He not alter those evil wills which He moves?" But, understandably if unsatisfactorily, Luther offers no answer: "It is not for us to inquire into these mysteries, but to adore them. If flesh and blood take offence here and grumble, well, let them grumble; they will achieve nothing; grumbling will not change God! And however many of the ungodly stumble and depart, the elect will remain. . . ." (*ibid.*, V, 6).

Nevertheless, from the fact that this is all monstrous, it does not follow either that this picture does not fairly represent the essentials of theism or that this is not after all our actual human situation. Less obviously, it would not be correct to say without qualification that, if God had made us innocent, then we should have been "innocent automata". This conclusion has often been drawn, and most respectably: ". . . as soon as it is assumed

that the Universal Primordial Being is the cause of the existence
of substance . . . Man would be a marionette or an automaton
. . . fabricated and wound up by the Supreme Artist. . . ."
(Kant (2), pp. 105–106).

Certainly, our relations to the Creator would then have
been more like those of a puppet to the puppetmaster, or the
automaton to its maker, than they would be like those of a
grown-up son to his father—or indeed any other relations
within the creation. Nevertheless just to say that then we would
be either puppets or automata is misleading. For it conceals the
truth, which Luther stressed, that the creation hypothesis
leaves all the observable features of the supposed creation
exactly as they were before. Notwithstanding that his own
conduct before the Diet of Worms provides the paradigm case
of the protestant hero—the man of principle who is supremely
no man's tool—it could still be true, as Luther himself believed,
that even then his choices and his every word and action were
determined by the Creator God: 'He's got the whole world in
his hands!'

In the previous subsection (5 (iv)), I argued that we can in
defence of fundamental known facts of immediate observation
entrench ourselves impregnably. We are now in a better
position to appreciate also the limitations of any such defence.[38]
Certainly no discovery, whether scientific or theological, could
ever show that there are not movings as well as motions, as
there defined. But then, unfortunately, this undeniable fact
cannot serve to show that the predestinarian nightmare is not
the hidden truth. Again, if words such as 'choice' and 'action'
are, as Compatibilists believe, definable on similar lines; then
there can equally be no possible doubt about the reality of their
referents either. But, of course, this provides no guarantee of the
reality of the postulated referents of any words which cannot
similarly be defined in terms of what is in fact observed. So if,
as Incompatibilists believe, the words in question cannot be so
defined, but contain also some controversial theoretical
content: then, as was urged in an earlier subsection (5 (ii)), it
must be doubtful whether human choice and human actions
are not, after all, fictions. But it is only and precisely in this
Incompatibilist understanding of choice and action, which I
hold to be a misunderstanding, that the reality of choice and

action must be, obviously and necessarily, incompatible with the predestinarian nightmare.

Again, although new discoveries cannot show that the known facts are not what they are, such discoveries may very well set those known facts into a very different perspective; and, when they are seen in that fresh perspective, a radical revaluation may be required. Thus we might have been so old-fashioned as to have thought it right that some delinquent should be punished: for he did not act " 'of compulsion' . . . but . . . spontaneously and voluntarily". Suppose now we learn that we are all, all the time, in all things, creatures of a Great Manipulator. Then—although it remains true that that particular delinquent acted, and not " 'under compulsion' . . . but . . . spontaneously and voluntarily"—we can no longer take it for granted that it would be right to punish him; and certainly not that it would be right for his Creator to become the Great Justiciar!

The upshot, therefore, is this. Aquinas, and Luther, and all the other classical theologians who were on the present philosophical issues Compatibilist, were in this quite right. Furthermore, as a matter of historical scholarship rather than of philosophy, the quotations from Aquinas and Luther in the previous subsection (5 (iv)) make it quite clear that the nightmare of the Great Manipulator is not—as perhaps most of us were mistakenly taught to think—the peculiarity of Calvin and Calvinism; but a necessary and immediate consequence of the essential theist doctrine of Divine creation.[39] Where all these theologians went wrong, I am suggesting, was in their drawing of normative conclusions. It is not so much their philosophy as their morals which were at fault!

The situation is different in the purely secular case, mentioned already in a previous subsection (5 (iii)). The difference is that in that case all human movings are supposed to be, not the movings at one remove of the Great Manipulator, but the latest outcomes of ultimately impersonal causes. Whereas in the former responsibility must at the very least be shared with, if not shifted wholly onto, the supposed Great Manipulator; in the latter there is and can be no one else to blame. In those finest and most characteristic words of Harry Truman: "The buck stops here!"

It can be argued that this difference is, or ought to be, crucial. Here I will only refer to what I said in that previous subsection about the possibility, and the desirability, of entrenching ourselves behind certain impregnable defences. Those enemies of traditional ideas and practices of account-ability who are so ill-advised as to attack these defences will be thrown back. They would be better advised—though I will not say well advised—to regroup, and to try to establish not that, science teaches, no one ever could in any sense do otherwise than he does, but that, in the new perspectives opened up by the progress of the human sciences, that whole array of distinctions provided for by our rich vocabulary of accountability, extenua-tion and excuse should be seen as far less important than has traditionally been thought.[40]

6. Causing and compelling

If his offensive is to succeed, and even if not, the Compatibilist must insist upon a realistic modesty in any formulation of scientific determinism. Spokesmen for the sciences, and above all for the psychological and social sciences, cannot be allowed to get away with rash, demonstrably false, claims that their disciplines presuppose or reveal a general truth which, if it were true, would be incompatible: not merely with, what they might understandably dismiss as a philosopher's will-of-the-wisp, libertarian free will; but also with what they of all people have no business to pretend is anything other than an inexpugnable psychological and social fact—the reality of human movings in which the agent always could in the more fundamental sense have done other than he did. (See Section 5 (iii); and compare Flew (4), VII 6.)

Consider how Plantinga, like so many others, makes doubly sure that Compatibilism shall appear "altogether paradoxical". Not only does he start by construing 'free will' as always and necessarily and by definition precluding universal causality. He also so defines 'causal determination' as to preclude all possibility of alternative action: "To say of Jones' Action A that it is causally determined is to say that the action in question has causes and that, given those causes, Jones could not have refrained from doing A" (*ibid.*, p. 133).

Certainly there is a sense of the word 'cause' in which to

cause an effect to happen must make the occurrence of that effect, once given the occurrence of that cause, inevitable. It is in that sense of 'cause' that Plantinga is here construing "Jones' action . . . is causally determined". That is also, I suggest, the normal sense of the word 'cause' when we are applying it to inanimate objects or to (most of) the brutes.

The usual sense in which we speak of a person being caused to do something is entirely different, and carries no incongruous, indeed incoherent, implication that the action thus caused was an occurrence which, in our fundamental sense, could not have been helped. In this second sense of 'cause' what "is caused is the free and deliberate act of a conscious and responsible agent, and 'causing him to do it' means affording him a motive for doing it" (Collingwood, p. 285). So when we say of a person that he "could not have refrained from doing A" this does not imply that the occurrence of A was inevitable. Instead, for reasons explained in Section 2 (iii), it presupposes that it was not. In the fundamental sense he could do otherwise, or could have done. But in fact he will not, or would not.

I have elsewhere argued more fully that this second, Collingwoodian, sense of 'cause' is central to all the sciences of man as man.[41] The causes discovered by these sciences are, therefore, such as presuppose rather than preclude the reality of choice and action. When we turn to our theological case yet a third notion is required. Clearly the theist must not and need not say that his God is the cause of everything which occurs; in the first, natural scientific, sense of 'cause'. He must not, because this would deny the manifest realities of choice and human action. He need not, because he can in another way maintain that "we receive from God not only the power of willing but its employment also" (5 (iv)), without thus exposing his whole system to immediate and decisive falsification. But he cannot simply say that God always causes His creatures to choose and to act as they do; in the second, Collingwoodian, sense of 'cause'. For typically, such Collingwoodian causing is immediately discernible by the agent thus provided with a motive.

What we need is a third sense of 'cause', which carries neither the implications of inevitability, which rightly belong to the first, nor these suggestions, which belong to the second, of the open providing of reasons as motives to an agent fully aware of what is going on. In this proposed third sense of 'cause' we could, without contradiction, say that another man, or God, might, by direct physiological manipulations, ensure that someone performs whatever actions that other man, or God, determines, and that the actions of this creature would nevertheless be genuine actions, such that it could always be truly said that in the fundamental sense he could have done otherwise than he did.

Such causing could not properly be assimilated to Luther's case of "a thief or a footpad being dragged off against his will to punishment" (5 (iv)). For that case, like mine of the missile man (2 (ii)), would involve only causing in the first sense. Nor, again, could it be properly assimilated to the standard case of compelling. For all such compulsion involves causing in the Collingwoodian sense; although it would, of course, be as wrong as in some circles it is common to take it that all Collingwoodian causing is compelling. Nevertheless, it would be absurd, even monstrous, to suggest that the person who is in this third way caused to decide thus rather than thus, instead of the person or the quasi-personal Being who caused him so to decide, ought to be called to account, perhaps to eternal account, for the sense of that decision. The outrage is inordinately compounded when it is further proposed that the manipulator, or the Great Manipulator, should be judge, jury, and executioner.

7. Conclusion

If, as I have myself been arguing, the Compatibilist is ultimately right; then the Free Will Defence offers no hope whatsoever of justifying the ways of God to man. But if this defence is to be developed in Incompatibilist terms, then the first problem is to show how these are to be squared with what so many if not all classical theologians have taken to be essentials of theism. For if we really were, and knew that we were, endowed with libertarian free will, then we should all possess a premise from which we should have to deduce, by an argument which both Aquinas and Luther themselves insisted to be valid, that such a Creator does not exist.

Part III
IMMORTALITY

CHAPTER 8

Philosophical Prolegomena to any Scientific Question of Survival

Bertrand Russell once wrote: "All the questions which have what is called a human interest—such, for example, as the question of a future life—belong, at least in theory, to special sciences and are capable, at least in theory, of being decided by empirical evidence . . . a genuinely scientific philosophy cannot hope to appeal to any except those who have the wish to understand, to escape from intellectual bewilderment . . . it does not offer, or attempt to offer, a solution to the problem of human destiny, or of the destiny of the Universe" (Russell (1), p. 28). The present chapter, indeed the whole of Part Three, can be seen as a critical commentary on this statement.

1. The enormous initial obstacle
There is a huge obstacle which lies across the path of any doctrine of personal survival or personal immortality. This enormous initial obstacle is perfectly obvious and perfectly familiar. Nevertheless, in order to put the whole discussion into the correct perspective, it is useful to begin by actually stating what it is. For only when this has been done shall we fully appreciate for what they are the three main sorts of ways of trying to circumvent or to overcome the obstacle; and only when this is appreciated shall we be able adequately to assess the success or failure of any such attempt.

Yet the vocabulary available for describing the obstacle may well be felt unfairly to prejudice the question against the believer in personal survival or personal immortality. To meet this difficulty I propose first to say and, hopefully, later to show that it is certainly not my intention to prejudge issues in this or any other way.

This huge obstacle lying across the path of any doctrine of personal survival or personal immortality is the familiar fact that—with the possible exceptions of the prophet Elijah and Mary the mother of Jesus bar Joseph—all men die and are in more or less short order buried, cremated, or otherwise disposed of. This universal fact of death is what leads us normally to distinguish after a shipwreck or an air crash, exclusively and exhaustively, between the Dead and the Survivors, with no third category of Both or Neither. This is the fact which gave the proposition 'All men are mortal' its hallowed status as the first premise of the stock traditional example of a valid syllogism; which proceeds from this and the further premise that 'Socrates is (or was) a man), to the true if unexciting conclusion that 'Socrates is (or was) mortal'.

2. Survival and immortality

Confronted by such an obstacle how is any such doctrine to get started? Before trying to suggest an answer I wish to make a sharp, simplifying move. I propose from now on to speak only of survival, without qualification, rather than of personal survival and personal immortality. I shall thus be taking it for granted, first, that what we are interested in is our personal post-mortem futures, if any. 'Survival' through our children and our children's children after we ourselves are irrecoverably dead, 'immortality' through the memories of others thanks to our great works, or even our immersion in some universal world-soul—whatever that might mean—may be as much as, or much more than, most of us will in fact be getting. And it may be lamentably self-centred, albeit humanly altogether understandable, that we should be concerned about more than these thin substitutes. But, for better or for worse, what we are discussing now is the possibility of our post-mortem survival as persons identifiable as those we are here and now.

I shall also be taking it for granted, second, that survival is the necessary though of course not the sufficient condition of immortality. We can and shall concentrate on survival because this is pre-eminently a case where it is the first step which counts. Immortality is just more of the same—survival for ever. This may seem another point too obvious to be worth making. I sympathise with this impatient reaction. But it is wrong. For

consider that the Roman Catholic Professor R. F. Holland
could write, in reviewing C. B. Martin's path-breaking study
Religious Belief, in *Mind* for 1961: "Christians believe that they
are to be resurrected. . . . They believe that they are in for
damnation or salvation. . . . The notion of 'looking forward to
life after death as a means of settling questions concerning the
existence and nature of God' . . . smacks of Spiritualism . . .
rather than Christianity" (p. 572).

3. Three ways for survival
We shall, therefore, have in mind always and only personal
survival; and we shall be concentrating on survival rather than
on immortality inasmuch as the former is the necessary but not
the sufficient first step to the latter. So, now, back to the question of how, granted the undeniable fact that we shall all die,
anyone can possibly maintain that some or all of us will
nevertheless survive. I distinguish three sorts of way in which
attempts can be, and have been, made to overcome this
enormous initial obstacle.

(i) The first and most familiar I call the Platonic or
Platonic-Cartesian way. This consists in two moves, not one.
The first move is to maintain that what is ordinarily thought of
as a person in fact consists of two radically disparate
elements: the one, the body, earthy, corporeal, and perishable;
the other, the soul, incorporeal, invisible, intangible, and
perhaps imperishable. The second move in the Platonic or
Platonic-Cartesian way consists in the contention that it is the
second of these two elements which is the real, essential person.
It is obvious that if this way will go, then what I call the
enormous initial obstacle is really no obstacle at all: the death
of the body is not necessarily the death of the soul, which is the
true person; and such an essentially incorporeal entity cannot
in principle be touched by the earthy corruptions of the
graveyard or the inferno of the crematorium. The case where
this soul is stipulated to be not incorporeal but corporeal I
classify as a special case of the second way, the way of the
astral body.

(ii) This second suggestion, like the first, consists in two
moves, not one. The first move is to claim that inside and, so
to speak, shadowing what is ordinarily thought of as the person

is another being of the same form. And the second move is, as before, to maintain that this shadow being is the real person. The crucial difference between the Platonic-Cartesian way and the way of the astral body is that, whereas in the former the soul is supposed to be essentially incorporeal, in the latter the astral body is equally essentially in its own way corporeal—albeit, of course, necessarily constituted of a different and somehow more shadowy and ethereal sort of stuff than familiar, workaday matter. Strictly speaking, it could not make sense to ask of a Platonic-Cartesian soul any such everyday and down-to-earth questions as 'Where is it?', 'How big is it?', 'How broad and long is it?'. Of the astral body, on the other hand, at least some such questions must be sensibly askable even if not in practice answerable, or what would be the point of talking of an astral body and not simply of a Platonic-Cartesian soul?

Once this crucial distinguishing point is grasped, the best method of increasing one's sympathetic understanding of the way of the astral body is to think of those stock cinematic representations—as long ago in the movie version of Noël Coward's *Blithe Spirit*—in which a shadow person, visible only sometimes and only to some of the characters, detaches itself from a person shown as dead and thereafter continues to participate in the developing action, at one time discernibly and at another time not.

This second way is not, I think, nowadays given the attention which it deserves. Part of the reason for this is that people familiar with the materials of psychical research have been persuaded to adopt a different interpretation of those apparitions of the living, the dying, and the dead which have to others seemed to provide the main prop for an astral body view (Tyrrell, passim). But partly, I suspect, the way of the astral body is simply ruled out of court as unacceptably crude or intolerably materialist; and this hasty dismissal is made all the easier by the assumption—which I shall soon be challenging—that there are no serious theoretical objections to the Platonic-Cartesian way.

(iii) The third of the three sorts of way which I want to distinguish and label finds its traditional home in religion rather than in psychical research. This is the one which I call the reconstitutionist way. The nature of this third way cannot be better shown than by quoting an epitaph composed for himself by Benjamin Franklin, Founding Father and Signer of the American Declaration of Independence. This epitaph has been erected not on but near his grave in Christ Church cemetery, Philadelphia, by the Poor Richard Society of that his city: "The body of B. Franklin, Printer, Like the Cover of an old Book, Its Contents torn out, And stript of its Lettering and Gilding, Lies here, Food for Worms. But the work shall not be lost; for it will, as he believ'd, appear once more in a new and more elegant Edition Corrected and improved By the Author."

4. Difficulties of the reconstitutionist way
The great, and surely quite decisive, difficulty here may be christened the Replica Objection. Consider a short but most revealing passage from Chapter XVII 'The Night Journey' in the *Koran*. As usual it is Allah speaking: "Thus shall they be rewarded: because they disbelieved our revelations and said, 'When we are turned to bones and dust shall we be raised to life?' Do they not see that Allah, who has created the heavens and the earth, has power to create their like? Their fate is preordained beyond all doubt. Yet the wrongdoers persist in unbelief."

Certainly Allah the omnipotent must have "power to create their like". But in making Allah talk in these precise terms of what He might indeed choose to do, the Prophet was speaking truer than he himself appreciated. For thus to produce even the most indistinguishably similar object after the first one has been totally destroyed and disappeared is to produce not the same object again, but a replica. To punish or to reward a replica, reconstituted on Judgement Day, for the sins or the virtues of the old Antony Flew dead and cremated in 1984 is as inept and as unfair as it would be to reward or to punish one identical twin for what was in fact done by the other. Again and similarly, the Creator might very well choose to issue a Second Edition—"Corrected and improved by the Author"—of Benjamin Franklin. But that Second Edition, however welcome, would by the same token not be the original Signer.

It was partly, though of course only partly, because he appreciated the force of this Replica Objection that Aquinas mixed a strong Platonic element into his version of the reconstitutionist way. The soul which could, and in his view did, survive death and wait for the reconstitution of the whole person on Judgement Day was for Aquinas only an incomplete fragment and not, as it was for Plato, the real and essential person. Yet this incomplete Thomist soul should, hopefully, be just enough to bridge the gap between now and then, and to provide sufficient necessary continuity between the Flew you see and the reconstituted Flew of Judgement Day to overcome the otherwise fatal Replica Objection.[42]

In Section 3 I deliberately distinguished all my three ways in ideal purity. But when we come to real cases we often find that the protagonist of what is predominantly one has been pressed by some difficulty to admit at least some element of another. Thus the primarily reconstitutionist Aquinas is driven to become in part a Platonist also. Later we shall see both how Plato himself, against all his wishes and intentions, lapses into an astral body view; and how the spokesman for an astral body in his turn may find himself so qualifying the nature of his elusive hypothesised body that it must become indistinguishable from a Platonic-Cartesian incorporeal soul.

5. *Difficulties of the Platonic way*
The first thing with which we must try to come to terms here is that the assumptions of the Platonic-Cartesian way, which in some contexts we find it so easy to make, are nevertheless both extraordinary and extraordinarily questionable.

(i) To appreciate how easy it is in some contexts to make these Platonic-Cartesian assumptions, consider a paper by the late Professor C. J. Ducasse, 'What would constitute conclusive evidence of survival after death?'. It was published in the *Journal of the Society for Psychical Research* for 1962. Ducasse supposes that our friend John Doe has been on board an aircraft which crashed in the ocean, and no survivors have been found. Our phone rings "and (*a*) a voice we recognise as John Doe's is heard and a conversation with it held which convinces us that the speaker is really John Doe . . . or (*b*) the voice heard is not John Doe's but that of some other person seemingly relaying his words to us and ours to him; and that the conversation so held does convince us that the person with whom we are conversing through that intermediary is John Doe" (p. 401). Ducasse continues: "Obviously, the two imagined situations (a) and (b) are, in all essentials, analogues of cases where a person is conversing with the purported surviving spirit of a deceased friend who either, in case (a), 'possesses' for the time being parts at least of the body of a medium . . . or else who, in case (b), employs the medium only as intermediary . . ." (pp. 401–402).

Now certainly this constitutes as clear and vivid a description as could be desired of the model in terms of which mediums and their sitters usually think of the proceedings of the seance room. Yet it is neither obvious nor true that "the two imagined situations . . . are, in all essentials, analogues" of the seance situation. The crucial difference lies in the fact that in the case of the imaginary plane crash we know only "that no survivors have been found", whereas in the seance case we presumably know, beyond any possibility of doubt, that our friend has indeed died, and that his remains have been duly buried, cremated, or in some other way consumed. Now Ducasse, in his own way, appreciated all this perfectly well. The reason why he did not see it as representing any difficulty at all for 'the survival hypothesis' is that here he, like almost everyone else when considering what is in psychical research called 'the survival evidence', took for granted a Platonic-Cartesian view of man.

These Platonic-Cartesian assumptions are made explicit a little later, when Ducasse continues: "Thus, because the John Doe case and the case of conversation through a medium are complete analogues, the particular kind of content of the conversation that would be adequate to prove or make positively probable that John Doe had survived the crash would likewise be adequate to prove or make positively probable that the mind of our deceased friend has survived the death of his body" (p. 402). This possibly surviving mind of Ducasse's is— as he himself, again in his own fashion, emphasizes—for our purposes nothing else but the Platonic-Cartesian soul: for it is an incorporeal entity which inhabits the body; and it is the real, essential person. Ducasse continues: "When the question of survival is formulated thus in terms not of 'spirits' but of *minds* then the allegation that the survival explanation makes gratuitously . . . four assumptions . . . is seen to be erroneous. For (a) that there are minds is not an assumption but a known fact; (b) that minds are capable of remembering is likewise not an assumption but is known; (c) that minds are capable of 'possessing' living human bodies is also a known fact, for 'possession' is but the name of the *normal* relation of a mind to its living body. *Paranormal* 'possession' would be possession in the very same sense, but only temporary, and of a living body by a mind other than its own—that other mind either being one which had been that of a body now dead; or being a mind temporarily wandering from its own living body. And (d) that telepathic communication between minds is possible is also a known fact" (p. 403: italics and inverted commas original).

(ii) Having shown by reference to Ducasse how easy and natural it is to make Platonic-Cartesian assumptions in the context of what is usually described as the survival evidence, the next thing is to challenge both these assumptions. What I shall now be doing is to develop, in a philosopher's way, a suggestion made many years ago by a leading American psychologist and psychical researcher, Gardner Murphy. Writing on 'Difficulties confronting the survival hypothesis' in the *Journal of the American Society for Psychical Research* for 1945 Murphy spoke of the "fact that bodies are the vehicles of personality, and that most people have no conception of personality except in such terms . . .". He challenged "the reader to try for a few minutes to imagine what his personal existence would be like if he were deprived of every device for making contact with his environment, except through the hypothetical use of continuous telepathy to and from other invisible minds" (p. 71).

I think that Murphy understated his case. For, surely, 'personality' is a term which has to be defined in terms of persons. My personality is some sort of function of my characteristics and my dispositions; and it could make no more sense to talk of my personality surviving my dissolution—of these characteristics existing without a me for them to be the characteristics of—than it would to talk of the grin of Carroll's Cheshire Cat outlasting the face of which it was one possible configuration. Nor is it just "most people", as Murphy modestly puts it, it is all of us whose conceptions of personality are grounded in the corporeal. For, as I have just said, personality is essentially some sort of function of persons; and persons are—surely equally essentially—corporeal.

Consider, for instance, how you would teach the meaning of any person word to a child. This is done, and I think could only be done, by some sort of direct or indirect pointing at members of that very special class of living physical objects to which we one and all belong. Or again, and slightly more subtly, consider some of the things which we easily and regularly say about people, and think how few, if any, of these things could be intelligibly said about incorporeal entities. We meet people, we shake hands with them, eat with them, see them, hear them; they get up, go to bed, sit down, smile, laugh, cry. All these activities, and many, many more, could only be predicated intelligibly of corporeal creatures.

Now look again at what Ducasse called the "known facts," and what I still want to call his Platonic-Cartesian assumptions. I agree, of course, that there are minds, provided that by this we mean only that such statements as that he has a first-rate mind, or that the child is developing a mind of his own, are often true. But these statements are, in the interpretation in which we know that they are often true, statements about the capacities and dispositions of flesh and blood people. They must not be misconstrued to imply that the people in question already possess, or are in the process of acquiring, important incorporeal components; much less that these—or any—people actually are incorporeal beings.

It is also perfectly true and much to the point to insist that all normal people are capable of a certain amount of remembering. But, to say that minds are the possessors of these capacities is either an oddly artificial and, it appears, highly misleading way of stating a fact about people, or else a speculative suggestion about a possible explanation of that same fact in terms of a hypothetical and, presumably, corporeal entity.

(iii) Suppose we were to grant that ESP is a reality, there is still absolutely no experimental reason to describe it as communication between minds or souls rather than as communication between people. Indeed, I believe that something even stronger and much more interesting might be said—something at which Murphy was perhaps hinting when he spoke a shade disrespectfully of "the hypothetical use of continuous telepathy to and from other invisible minds". For could such bodiless beings, necessarily lacking all conventional sensory equipment, properly be said to communicate with one another by ESP, or even singly to possess any ESP capacity? And, if they could, could they be said to know that they were thus communicating, or that they did possess such a capacity?

These questions arise—although I cannot recall having heard them put before—because the term 'ESP' is, whether implicitly or explicitly, defined negatively by reference to the absence or neglect of all ordinary and ultimately perceptual methods of acquiring and communicating information; and because it is only by reference at some stage to the conventional sources that we become able to identify authentic ESP experiences or performances as being truly such; and thus to distinguish these both from acquisitions of information through normal channels and from such autonomous features of our own lives as our spontaneous and not significantly veridical imaginings. We never should forget, what too often is forgotten, that 'ESP' is not the name of some directly identifiable means of information transfer. Indeed, despite the close resemblance between the words 'telepathy' and 'telephony', any performance depending on telephony or any other such known and normal means is for that very reason at once disqualified as a case of telepathy; and the same applies, with appropriate alterations, as regards clairvoyance. Nor can authentic ESP experiences be picked out as such simply by reference to the strong conviction of the subject that this is the real thing. It is, or should be, notorious that subjective conviction is not a sufficient condition of either normal or paranormal knowledge: I may with complete confidence and absolute sincerity claim either to know normally or to have exercised my supposed ESP capacity, and yet in fact be totally mistaken. We must, therefore, distinguish: between (a) in fact possessing or exercising some ESP capacity, whether or not you believe or know that you do or are; (b) believing that you possess or are exercising an ESP capacity, whether or not you in fact do or are; and (c) genuinely knowing—as opposed to believing with however little warrant or however mistakenly—that you do possess or perhaps actually are exercising such a capacity.

Suppose now that in the light of these reminders we try to apply ESP concepts to these putative incorporeal subjects of experiences. Suppose further that it is a fact that there actually is some close correspondence between the mental contents of two such hypothetical bodiless beings, although such a fact would not, surely, be known by any normal means by anyone—whether bodied or bodiless. Now how could either of these bodiless beings have, how indeed could there even be, any reason for saying that this close correspondence must point to some information transfer from one to the other? How could either of these bodiless beings have—indeed how could there even be—any reason for holding that some of its mental contents must have been intruded by, or otherwise correspond with, some of those of another similarly bodiless being; and some particular one, at that? How could either have, indeed how could there be, any good reason for picking out some of its mental contents as—so to speak—messages received, for taking these but not those as the expressions of an exercise not of imagination but of ESP? Fundamentally similar difficulties arise when we attempt to apply ESP concepts to the different cases of information transfer between an ordinary person and a supposed bodiless being, and between material things and such a being (telepathy from the living to a spirit, that is, and clairvoyance by a spirit). The upshot appears to be that the concepts of ESP are essentially parasitical upon everyday and this-worldly notions; that where there could not be the normal, there could not be ESP as the exception to that rule.

It is too often and too easily assumed that ESP capacities could be, or even must be, the attributes of something altogether immaterial and incorporeal; partly for no better reason than that they do indeed seem to be non-physical in the entirely different sense of being outside the range of today's physical theories. Yet the truth appears to be that the very concepts of ESP are just as much involved with the human body as are those of other human capacities. It was this point which Wittgenstein was making, with regard to our normal and known attributes and capacities rather than anything putative or paranormal, when he said gnomically: "The human body is the best picture of the human soul" (Wittgenstein (2), p. 178).

(iv) We have no business, therefore, simply to take a

Platonic-Cartesian view of man for granted; and to proceed at once to the question of whether the so-called survival evidence is in fact sufficient to establish that we, in our putative essential natures as incorporeal souls, do survive death and the dissolution of our bodies. Before we can possibly become entitled to begin to construe that material as evidence for this conclusion a great deal of work will have to be done to show: (a) that there can be a coherent notion of an incorporeal personal being; and (b) that a being of this sort could significantly and truly be said to be the same person as he was when he was a creature of flesh and blood.

My own conviction is that no amount of work can turn these two tricks. It is surely significant that Plato himself—an imaginative writer of genius as well as the Founding Father of philosophy—when he came at the end of his *Republic* to describe in the Myth of Er the life of supposedly incorporeal souls, was quite unable to say anything about them which did not presuppose that they must be, after all, in some fashion corporeal. So, against all his wishes and intentions, Plato there lapsed from his own eponymous position into what was in effect an astral body view.

(v) But, suppose we take Plato's own failure in the Myth of Er—as, surely, he would have done had it been pointed out to him—as showing only that our vocabulary and our imagination are deplorably limited by our present, but temporary, enmeshment in the body. And suppose we concede—as surely we must—that the person words of our present vocabulary do not refer to incorporeal souls, but to creatures of all too solid flesh. Can we not develop a new and coherent concept of an incorporeal being to whom at least some of the characteristics presently ascribed to people could also significantly be attributed? I do not think that we can. The basic difficulties are, first, to provide a principle of individuation by which one such being could, at least in theory, be distinguished from another such being; and, second, to provide a principle of identity to permit us to say that one such being at a later time is the same as that being at an earlier time.

This is difficult ground, though we can get much help by considering the unsuccessful labours of Descartes and his successors. Since they mistook it that people are incorporeal subjects of experience, our problem appeared to them not as one of developing a coherent new notion, but as that of giving an account of our present notion of a person. But this does not make their efforts any less relevant to us. The first thing which emerges is that such an incorporeal personal being will have to be conceived as consisting of a series of conscious experiences—along, no doubt, with some dispositions, inclinations, and capacities. In the light of what has been argued already in a previous subsection (5 (iii)), we have to add that unless we can solve the theoretical problem of attributing ESP and other putative paranormal capacities to such a being, these dispositions and so on will have to refer exclusively to actual or possible members of the same series of experiences. We now have a choice between two options: either, with Descartes, we attribute these experiences to an incorporeal spiritual substance—the I in Descartes' claim "I am a thinking substance"; or else, with Hume, we say that we can make nothing of the idea of such a substance and then go on to say that such an incorporeal being must simply consist in a series of experiences.

Neither alternative shows promise. Take the second first. Whatever difficulties there may be about the idea of a substance characterised as incorporeal, it should be easy to see why some substance is required. The word 'substance' is being used here in its main—not, alas, its only—philosophical sense. In this sense a substance is that which can significantly be said to exist separately and in its own right, so to speak. Any experience requires a substance to be the experience of in exactly the same way that a grin requires a face to be the grin of. Since it makes no sense to talk of a pain or a joy or any other sort of awareness without an owner, Hume's suggestion in the *Treatise* (I (iv) 6) that a person might simply and solely consist in a collection of such "loose and separate" experiences must be rated as, strictly, nonsense.

Hume himself never seems to have realised that and why this suggestion cannot do. But he did soon see, and confessed in the Appendix, that there is no available string, no uniting principle, to bind any such collection together and to distinguish it from any other. The obvious candidate might seem to be memory, as Locke had suggested earlier in his *Essay* (II (xxvii)). For, surely, we are inclined to think, the person himself must always be able—if only he would tell us, and would tell us true—to say whether it was in fact he or another who had the thought or did the deed. But this, as we shall see in Chapter Ten, will not work.

Expressed in modern terms, there is no possibility of giving an account of the self-identity and individuation of incorporeal collections of experiences in terms of their memory capacities. Certainly if I truly remember, and do not merely seem to remember, doing the deed, then necessarily I must be the same person as did that deed: true memory thus presupposes true personal identity. But what I remember is that I am the same person as did the deed. That I do so remember is not, and cannot be, itself what it is for me to be the same person as did it.

So what about the Cartesian alternative? Can we accept that an incorporeal person would be the incorporeal substance which enjoyed or suffered certain experiences, and was endowed with certain capacities? The principle of individuation would then be a matter of being, or belonging to, one such substance rather than to another; and the principle of self-identity would be a matter of being, or belonging to, the same such substance.

But now, before we discuss the qualifications of this candidate, can we be told who (or what) he (or it) is? For when we were dealing with regular or conventional (corporeal) persons, there was no difficulty in saying—indeed, in showing—what was the substance to which we were attributing the experiences, the dispositions, etc.: they were the experiences, the dispositions, or whatever, of a flesh and blood person. But what positive characterisation can we give to these postulated incorporeal substances? Can we say anything to differentiate such an incorporeal substance from an imaginary, an unreal, a non-existent substance?: "Beyond the wholly empty assurance that it is a metaphysical principle which guarantees continuing identity through time, or the argument that since we know that identity persists some such principle must hold in default of others, no content seems available for the doctrine. Its irrelevance . . . is due to its being merely an alleged identity-guaranteeing condition of which no independent characterisation is forthcoming" (Penelhum, p. 76).

6. *Difficulties in the way of the astral body*

The great, and in my view insuperable, difficulties of the Platonic way, the assumptions of which have so often been taken for granted or even asserted as known facts, should now lead us to look with a new interest and respect at the way of the astral body.

In the context of this more sympathetic approach, it begins to emerge that many of those who have been thought of as— and who probably thought themselves—Platonic-Cartesians have really been believers in astral bodies. There is, for instance, some reason to think that the Latin Father Tertullian, who certainly held the soul to be corporeal, was also inclined to think of it as of human shape; and what is this but an astral body? See Chapter IX of his *de Anima*, in which he cites the visions of the good sister who saw "a soul in bodily shape . . . in form resembling that of a human being in every respect". Tertullian then goes on to argue that such an object must have a colour, which could be no other than an "ethereal transparent one".

Since we come to examine this notion of an astral body so soon after deploying the objection to the candidate notion of incorporeal spiritual substance, it will be easy to see what the problem for the protagonist is going to be. It is, obviously, to find some positive characterisation for an astral body: such that an astral body really would be a sort of body in a way in which an imaginary body, or a non existent body, or an incorporeal body are not sorts of body; and at the same time such that the hypothesis that we have, or are, astral bodies is not shown to be false by any presently available facts. Confronted by this problem, the danger for the protagonist of an astral body view is that in his concern to avoid immediate falsification by presently known facts he may so qualify the nature of the body which he wants to hypothesize that it becomes in effect not a body, albeit elusive, but instead an incorporeal Platonic-Cartesian soul: "A fine brash hypothesis may thus be killed by inches, the death by a thousand qualifications."

In principle these dangers could, I think, be escaped fairly easily. We should need only to postulate the detectability of astral bodies by an instrument of a kind not yet invented. But such an utterly arbitrary postulation would invite the comment made by Bertrand Russell in another connection: "The method of 'postulating' what we want has many advantages; they are the same as the advantages of theft over honest toil" (Russell (2), p. 21). Such a drastic postulation would be warranted only if we thought—or think—that the survival evidence cannot be interpreted in terms of various ESP ongoings among ordinary corporeal people, and if we also believe—as I have been arguing that we should—that the Platonic-Cartesian way will not go. It would also be much encouraged if evidence for levitating, apporting, and generally rip-roaring physical mediumship were better than it is.

7. Tentative conclusions on the substantive question

Certainly I cannot myself recommend the reckless postulation which would be required in order to proceed along the way of the astral body. For I remain persuaded by the sort of considerations deployed so long ago by Professor E. R. Dodds in his 'Why I do not believe in survival', in the *Proceedings of the Society for Psychical Research* for 1934. The crux of this landmark paper, which ought to be reprinted in some more accessible and more widely circulating form, is that the so-called survival evidence can be adequately, and therefore better interpreted in terms of more or less elaborate and unconscious normal and paranormal transactions among the living—without postulating any surviving entities at all. Substantially the same conclusion was reached by Murphy in the paper mentioned in Section 5 (ii). (Compare too Flew (1) Chapter VII.) If, however, I were to take the opposite view to that of Dodds and Murphy on this issue, as many do, then I should have to postulate some sort of astral body; and that notwithstanding the rather formidable difficulties indicated in the previous Section 6. For these difficulties, unlike those of the supposed hypothesis of disembodied survival, do not necessarily reduce the proposed postulate to incoherence. My conclusion is, therefore, that if there is to be a case for individual and personal survival, what survives must be some sort of astral body; but that, in the present state of the evidence, we have no need of that hypothesis.

CHAPTER 9

Can a Man Witness his own Funeral?

1. Reinforcing the challenge to Platonic-Cartesian assumptions

In Section 3 (i) of Chapter Eight I defined "the Platonic or Platonic-Cartesian way" as consisting in "two moves. The first move is to maintain that what is ordinarily thought of as a person in fact consists of two radically disparate elements: the one, the body, earthy, corporeal, and perishable; the other, the soul, incorporeal, invisible, intangible, and perhaps imperishable. The second move . . . consists in the contention that it is the second of these two elements which is the real, essential person". In Section 5 of Chapter Eight I outlined the main reasons for thinking "that the assumptions of the Platonic-Cartesian way, which in some contexts we find it so easy to make, are nevertheless both extraordinary and extraordinarily questionable".

In the present Chapter Nine, and in Chapter Ten, I shall be reinforcing the challenge to these assumptions. Here it will be mainly a matter of underlining, in a rather piquant and dramatic context, the truth and significance of the point made in Section 5 (ii) of Chapter Eight: the point that our whole vocabulary for talking about people is, and has to be, explained by reference to—even defined in terms of—those corporeal creatures of flesh and blood which we seem to be— and surely are. When this point is fully seized, but only then, it will become clear just how unpromising is the second of the two moves required if the Platonic-Cartesian way is to be made to go. In Chapter Ten I shall be developing part of the case sketched in Section 5 (v) of Chapter Eight: the case, that is, for concluding that there could not be a viable concept of a Platonic-Cartesian soul; because there is no way in which such an entity could be identified and individuated. If this appropriately tentative conclusion is right, then neither the first nor consequently the second of the two moves of the Platonic-Cartesian way are possible.

Both Chapter Nine and Chapter Ten retraverse some portions of ground crossed already in Chapter Eight. This is a good thing. Platonic-Cartesian assumptions are far too deeply and far too strongly entrenched to be overrun in one single impetuous onslaught. In Section 5 (i) of the previous chapter we saw how C. J. Ducasse, who was both a sophisticated philosopher and a leading member of the American Society for Psychical Research, took these assumptions absolutely for granted as known truths. It is similarly remarkable that in England too H. H. Price, who is also both a very sophisticated philosopher and a leading member of the parallel (British) Society for Psychical Research, does exactly the same—altogether unworried, it seems, that these assumptions can be and are challenged by serious and well-girded critics. Thus in a paper on 'Survival and the Idea of "Another World" ', first published in the *Proceedings of the S.P.R.*, but now more easily accessible in the collection by J. R. Smythies on *Brain and Mind* to which I here refer, Price writes: "It is easy enough to conceive (whether or not it is true) that experiences might occur after Jones' death which are linked with experiences which he had before his death, in such a way that his personal identity is preserved." The objection which Price then goes on to consider is this: "But, it will be said, the idea of after-death *experiences* is just the difficulty. What kind of experiences could they conceivably be?" (p. 3: italics original).

Certainly, the crucial question is the one about the possibility of after-death experiences. It is this and only this which gives the question of a future life its enormous human interest:

> . . . Who would fardels bear,
> To grunt and sweat under a weary life,
> But that the dread of something after death,
> The undiscovered country, from whose bourn
> No traveller returns—puzzles the will,
> And makes us rather bear those ills we have
> Than fly to others that we know not of?
> Thus conscience doth make cowards of us all
> *(Hamlet* III (i)).

But prior to the difficulty to which Price devotes himself there is another and more fundamental one. Before any question can arise about the object or content of experiences, there has to be some subject to which these experiences can be attributed. It would, as I have urged before, make no more sense to talk of experiences without anyone to have them than it does to speak of a grin without a face to grin it. Price, of course, does not speak of experiences in this way. But he avoids this only by always taking it for granted that people are essentially incorporeal. The question then for Price is: 'What experiences could be had by such subjects if they survived the dissolution of their bodies?' In making this Platonic-Cartesian assumption of personal incorporeality, Price sets himself within a great and ancient tradition. It is, nevertheless, a tradition which starts from the wrong place, and which thereby stands every issue upon its head.

2. An attempted philosophical fool's mate
Suppose, once again, that the Survivalist says: 'We all of us survive death'; or: 'We all of us live for ever'. And suppose, this time, that the Mortalist plays naive: 'Whatever in the world do you mean? For, in the ordinary senses of the words you use, the former sentence expresses a self-contradiction, while the latter denies one of the most securely established of all empirical generalisations.' Since the Mortalist's objections to the two utterances of the Survivalist are different, let us consider them separately and in turn.

(i) 'We all of us survive death' is self-contradictory, because we use the words 'death' and 'survival' and their derivatives in such a way that the classification of the crew of a torpedoed ship into Dead and Survivors is both exclusive and exhaustive: every member of the crew, that is to say, must (logical 'must') have either died or survived; and no member of the crew could (logical 'could') have both died and survived.

It is easy to overlook the self-contradiction because it is our normal, sensibly cooperative, practice to give such strictly incorrect utterances the benefit of the doubt. Generously, and usually rightly, we assume that other people, like ourselves, have something intelligible to express even when they speak or write in incorrect ways. We attempt to attach some sense even to expressions which are strictly self-contradictory. This sympathetic tendency is frequently exploited by those who are competing for our attention. Posters advertising the film *Bachelor Husband* catch the eye precisely because the expression 'bachelor husband' is thus strictly self-contradictory. The title holds us. We puzzle over it. We ponder—perhaps to the advertiser's eventual profit—the possible non-linguistic improprieties suggested by this linguistically improper expression.

Similarly, if we see the headline, 'We survived death!', we do not just exclaim (in the tone of voice of rigid logical schoolmasters): 'Nonsense: you either survive or you die!' Instead, curiosity aroused, we read on to learn how the death was only 'death' (in inverted commas), that the people in question had only pretended, been reported, appeared, to die; but had not of course in fact died. Sometimes, for instance, people show all the usual 'symptoms' of death, all the usually reliable signs that they will not walk, or talk, or joke again, but then, surprisingly, recover and do walk and talk and joke once more. This happened quite often in the Second World War. Russian doctors in particular reported many cases of patients who showed the usual indications of death—the heart not beating, and so forth—but were brought back to life by shock treatments, blood transfusions, and suchlike. These patients thus survived 'death' (in inverted commas). The doctors then adapted their language—or at least the language of *Soviet War News* (London) was adapted—to meet the new situation. The phrase, 'We cannot survive death', was retained as the expression of a necessary truth. But the expression 'clinical death' was introduced as a more precise and less awkward substitute for 'death' (in inverted commas), in order to refer to the condition of those patients who showed all the usual, so to speak, symptoms of death but who nevertheless might or might not go on later to tell the tale. The expression, 'We all of us survive death', thus always was, and remains, strictly self-contradictory.

Neither the paradoxical employments of this and similar expressions, nor the inverted-comma usage of the word 'death' in which people can be said to return from the 'dead' (in inverted commas), weigh against this contention. On the contrary, they presuppose it. It is precisely and only because

'He survived death' is self-contradictory that it makes a good headline. It is precisely and only because 'to survive death' is self-contradictory that the doctors put the word 'death' between warning inverted commas when they first had to report that a patient survived 'death' (in inverted commas); and that they later introduced the new alternative expression 'clinical death'. The case resembles, but is not the same as that of the evidence of our own eyes, mentioned in Section 4 (ii) of Chapter One. For the phrase 'the evidence of my own eyes' has the force which it has precisely and only because to see with your own eyes is—usually—to have better than the best of evidence.

(ii) 'We all of us live for ever', on the other hand, is not self-contradictory but just as a matter of fact false. For it is the flat contrary of the massively confirmed empirical generalisation that all men are mortal.

Here we have perhaps to notice that 'All men are mortal' has sometimes been construed in other ways: the appropriate response in these different interpretations will be different. Some have read it, for instance, as meaning only that all human beings are naturally liable to death. This reading had what seemed to them the advantage of permitting the proposition 'All men are mortal' to remain unfalsified by the supposed bodily assumptions of the prophet Elijah and Mary the mother of Jesus bar Joseph.[43] For these elevations would have been not natural but miraculous. Others have read the same form of words as expressing not a would-be factual generalisation but a made-to-measure truth of logic, the word 'man' being interpreted as meaning a creature of a certain always mortal kind. This reading necessarily carries the not universally welcome implication that the prophet Elijah and Mary the mother of Jesus bar Joseph, always assuming that they did not die but were thus miraculously translated, cannot rate as human beings at all. If Mary was not human, then goodbye to any orthodox Christian doctrine of the Incarnation.

3. A possible counter to this attempt

One of many moves which might be made against the philosophical fool's mate attempted by the Mortalist in Section 2 is to reply that 'We all of us survive death' cannot be self-contradictory, and therefore incoherent, because it refers to a possibility which is not merely conceivable but also imaginable. What is conceivable is what is not self-contradictory and what it makes sense to say. What is imaginable is, here, whatever we can form a mental image of.[44] The classic illustration of this distinction was provided by Descartes in his fifth *Meditation*:

> But I cannot image the thousand sides of a chiliagon as I do the three sides of the triangle. . . . And although . . . it may happen that in conceiving a chiliagon I do confusedly represent some figure to myself; still it is very clear that this figure is not a chiliagon, since it does not differ at all from the one which I should represent to myself if I were thinking of a myriagon or of some other figure with an abundance of sides.

Let us waive the point that Descartes's argument as just quoted actually proves not that he could not image a chiliagon, but that, even if he did, he could not know whether and when he had. For the latter is in any case sufficient, while our present concern is with the contention that our survival after death is not merely conceivable but also imaginable. One distinguished protagonist of this contention was Moritz Schlick, chairman of the old original Vienna Circle of Logical Positivists. His statement first appeared in *The Philosophical Review* for 1936:

> I take it for granted that . . . we are concerned with the question of survival after 'death'. I think we may agree with Professor C. I. Lewis when he says about this hypothesis: 'Our understanding of what would verify it has no lack of clarity. In fact I can easily imagine, e.g., witnessing the funeral of my own body and continuing to exist without a body, for nothing is easier than to describe a world which differs from our ordinary world only in the complete absence of all data which I would call parts of my own body. We must conclude that immortality, in the sense defined, should not be regarded as a metaphysical 'problem', but is an empirical hypothesis, because it possesses logical verifiability. It could be verified by following the prescription 'Wait until you die!' (p. 356).

Two things are worth mentioning right away. First, it was Schlick himself who inserted those giveaway inverted commas round the word 'death' in his first sentence. They constitute a tacit admission that the expression 'to survive death' is indeed self-contradictory. Compare the similar tacit concession in the tombstone protest: 'Not dead, but sleeping'. Second, Schlick personally had no Survivalist longings. So if we see, as we do, that he too is taking the assumptions of the Platonic-Cartesian way absolutely for granted, this constitutes further very good evidence of the strength and persistence of those assumptions. Compare then the even more remarkable case of Hume, mentioned in Section 5 (v) of Chapter Eight. Although Hume was, and wanted to be, a Mortalist; and although he had eventually to confess himself at a loss to give any coherent account of the identity of persons, conceived as incorporeal; still his rather self-conscious radicalism in the *Treatise* went no further here than to challenge, with unfortunate results, the notion of the person as an incorporeal substance. With everything to gain and nothing to lose, even Hume, "the all-destroyer",[45] never thought to deny the bizarre assumption that people are essentially incorporeal.

To continue: a briefer, more puckish, and less categorical version of Schlick's contention is briefly entertained in John Wisdom's unending saga *Other Minds*: "But it doesn't follow that the man doesn't exist anywhere, disembodied or in a new body. It is 'I shall be dead tomorrow' in this disembodied sense, which provides 'a first-class puzzle for the positivists'. For how could it be verified? I know indeed what it would be like to witness my own funeral—the men in tall silk hats, the flowers, and the face beneath the glass-topped coffin" (p. 36). A third, less colourful version can be found in Casimir Lewy's 'Is the Notion of Disembodied Existence Self-Contradictory?' in the *Proceedings of the Aristotelian Society* for 1942–43 (pp. 64–65).

4. The counter countered

So far as I know, the particular contention of Section 3, with its explicit appeal to what can be imagined, had never been attacked in print before the first publication of the paper on which the present chapter is based. Presumably everyone could imagine (image) a scene such as Wisdom describes, and anyway no one wanted to seem to arrogate to himself the right to say what Wisdom or Schlick or anyone else other than himself could or could not imagine (image). Schlick's contention nevertheless can and should be challenged, and the challenge can be pressed home without arbitrarily presuming to draw limits to Wisdom's obviously considerable imaginative powers.

The crux is that there is a world of difference between: on the one hand, imagining what it would be like to witness my own funeral; and, on the other hand, imagining what it would be like *for me* to witness my own funeral. What Schlick and Wisdom and everyone else can certainly do is the former. What would be needed to warrant Schlick's conclusions is the latter. The question at issue is a question about possible pictures and possible captions; and it helps to follow Wittgenstein's general advice to think of public physical pictures rather than private mental images.[46] Everyone knows what picture fits the first caption. What picture is it which fits, and justifies, the second caption?

If it is really I who witness, then it is not my funeral but only 'my funeral' (in inverted commas). If it really is my funeral, then I cannot be a witness; since I shall be dead and in the coffin. Of course I can imagine (image) what might be described as my watching 'my own funeral' (in inverted commas). I can remember Harry Lime in the film *The Third Man* watching 'his own funeral' and of course I can imagine being in the same situation as Harry Lime. But it was not really Harry Lime's own funeral, and what I can imagine would not really be mine. Again I can imagine my own funeral—I shall not try to better Wisdom's whimsical description of such a scene. But now what I am imagining is not my witnessing my own funeral but merely my own funeral.

It is interesting to notice that, just as Schlick gave his point away by his nicely sensitive insertion of the required inverted commas round the word 'death', so Wisdom likewise is too careful a stylist to allow one of his characters to describe his imaginings in the terms needed to support Schlick's philosophical thesis. What Wisdom wrote was: "I know indeed what it would be like to witness my own funeral." But this does nothing to support the Schlick thesis. What that requires is that he should be able to imagine his surviving his own death and his witnessing his own funeral. For it is this which Schlick's opponent maintains is a self-contradictory and hence strictly incoherent suggestion.

But surely this is merely cheap and flash? Surely I can perfectly well imagine my own funeral, really my own funeral with my body in the coffin and not a substitute corpse or a weight of bricks; with me there watching it all, but invisible, intangible, a disembodied spirit? Well, yes, this seems all right—until someone asks the awkward question: 'Just how does all this differ from your imagining your own funeral without your being there at all (except as the corpse in the coffin)?'

Certainly Schlick could imagine, as he claimed, "the funeral of his own body", although it is perhaps a pity that he should describe what he imagined in this way and not, more naturally, as his own funeral. But then he goes on to talk of imagining his "continuing to exist without a body", which he tries to justify by claiming that "nothing is easier than to describe a world which differs from our ordinary world only in the complete absence of all data which I would call parts of my own body". But the fact that we can all of us describe, or even imagine, a world which would differ from our ordinary world only in the complete absence of all data describable as parts of our respective bodies has not, by itself, the slightest tendency to show that anyone could imagine or describe a world in which, after his funeral, he continued to exist without a body. By itself it merely shows that we can each imagine what the world would be like if he were obliterated from it entirely, and no trace of his corpse remained. Schlick has misdescribed what he could imagine. Misled by the fact that a man can easily imagine what his funeral will be like, and hence what it would be like to watch it, it is tempting to insist that he can imagine what it would be like *for him* to watch his own funeral. Schlick is thus able to "conclude that immortality, in the sense defined . . . is an empirical hypothesis. . . . It could be verified by following the prescription 'Wait until you die!' " But he has not defined a sense of 'immortality' at all. He has merely misdescribed some rather humdrum exercises of his imagination in an extremely exciting and misleading way. He has failed to say anyting to prevent his opponent from objecting to his conclusion: 'But, on the contrary, nothing whatever could be verified (by me) by (my) following the prescription "Wait until you die!": (for me my) death is so final that it is logically impossible (for me) to survive it to verify any hypotheses at all.'

5. Conclusions

Of course, this is not, and ought not to be, the end of the affair. But it does at least get us back to the heart of the matter. What the move of Section 3, and the counter-move of Section 4, do bring out more clearly is that no one has any business simply to assume a Platonic-Cartesian view of man; and then to proceed to inquire what reason there may be for believing that the incorporeal beings, which we thus supposedly are, survive, either temporarily or for ever, the dissolution of their corporeal containers. Just as I argued in Chapter One that wherever our inquiries about God should rightly end, they ought to begin from the defeasible presumption of atheism; so I have throughout Part Three been urging that, wherever our inquiries about personal survival or personal immortality should in truth end, they ought to start from the defeasible presumption that people are creatures of flesh and blood.

It is scarcely possible to deny that person words—and indeed that whole large section of our vocabulary which we employ primarily or exclusively to say things about people— are, and have to be, taught by reference to such corporeal beings. So the onus of proof must surely be on those who want to maintain that, all this notwithstanding, people really are essentially incorporeal. By 'person words' I here mean those words—such as 'father', 'I', 'man', 'person', or 'butcher'— which are employed to refer to people. When I speak of "that whole large section of our vocabulary which we employ primarily or exclusively to say things about people" I have in mind such expressions as 'thinks about socialism', 'feels jealous of', 'expresses his egalitarian ideals', and innumerable others. In this present case I find even more difficulty than I did in the first in pretending to believe that there is any live possibility of the defeasible presumption being in fact defeated.

Having said all this, it is important to emphasise that I have most carefully not said that these words refer merely to, or are defined in terms of, bodies. 'Person' is no synonym for (human) 'body'. For though 'bodies' was in my day employed in the Services as a slightly contemptuous substitute for 'people', the degrading point of that substitution would have been lost had the words really been synonymous. Again, there is a difference —a matter of life and death—between on the one hand, 'We brought a body down from the foot of the Z'mutt ridge', and, on the other hand, 'We brought a woman down from the foot of the Z'mutt ridge'. Consider this item under the heading, "Climber killed by avalanche", from the London *Times*: "Five mountaineers were trapped by an avalanche yesterday.... Two escaped. Two others were extricated by an R.A.F. Mountain Rescue squad. . . . Mr. N. Ryder . . . was buried under several feet of snow and another rescue party located his body early this morning" (3 January 1951).

Person words do not, therefore, mean either bodies or souls, nor yet any combination of the two; and the defeasible presumption that people are creatures of flesh and blood is not to be confounded with either of these two different, and both mistaken, claims. The word 'I' is no synonym for 'my body', nor 'my mind' nor 'my soul', nor for any combination of the two; as any doubter who tries a few substitutions will quickly discover for himself. If we are indeed compound of two such disparate elements, then that is a contingent fact about people and not part of what is meant by 'person' and other person words. To suggest that it has been assumed that people are merely bodies is to reveal that you yourself assume that everyone must be a dualist, or at least a dualist with one component missing—a sort of one-legged dualist. And this is wrong.

I

CHAPTER 10

The Identity of Incorporeal Persons

1. *Preamble*

In Section 2 of Chapter Nine the argument was put that, in the most ordinary senses of the words involved, 'We all of us survive death' is self-contradictory, while 'We all of us live for ever' is the flat contrary of what is known by all to be as a matter of fact the truth. In Sections 3 and 4 of the same chapter we examined, and found good reason to discount, one plausible response to this attempt by the Mortalist at a philosophical fool's mate. Another, alternative move would be to urge that, although Schlick's plausible response was after all misconceived, still it is easy to attach new senses to the same words, such that the first apparently decisive objections no longer hold. And of course this is true.

But, as I insisted in Section 2 of Chapter Eight, our concern is with only some of these possible new senses. We are not concerned, for instance, with the possibility of talking of survival through our children and our children's children, or through the memories of others, after we ourselves are finally and irrecoverably dead. We have no business here with any sense or possible sense of 'survival' or 'immortality' except in so far as the news that we were, in this sense, to survive or to be immortal would justify us in cherishing Wisdom's "logically unique expectations . . . expectations as to what one will see and feel after death" (Flew (Ed.) (1), p. 188). It is in this understanding, and in this understanding alone, that we can echo the much quoted words of Bishop Butler. His Dissertation 'Of Personal Identity' opens: "Whether we are to live in a future state, as it is the most important question which can possibly be asked, so it is the most intelligible one which can be expressed in language."

Where Butler is altogether mistaken is when in his very next sentence he proceeds to complain: "Yet strange perplexities have been raised about the meaning of that identity or sameness of person, which is implied in the notion of our living now and hereafter, or in any two successive moments". For, from the fact that we can understand and share the human interest of the "logically unique expectation", it does not follow that any presuppositions of the truth of that expectation must be mutually consistent. We can, for instance, understand and feel remorse: the longing, not merely to reverse the actual consequences of what we have done, but also actually to secure that we should not have done what we have done. Yet the past is by definition unalterable; and so the suggestion that we might thus literally undo what we have done must be, if anything is, incoherent and self-contradictory. Butler was, therefore, mistaken when he inferred from the intelligibility of the "logically unique expectation", and from its outstanding human interest, that there can be no difficulties about what "is implied in the notion of our living now and hereafter, or in any two successive moments".

In fact there are difficulties, intractable difficulties. For what is so implied is that there are—and we are—Platonic-Cartesian souls. There are indeed difficulties, though surely not intractable difficulties, about giving an adequate philosophical account of personal identity when the word 'person' is taken to refer to a kind of familiar corporeal object; when—to coin a slogan—'People are what you meet'. But, by defining the scope of his inquiry into "the meaning of . . . identity or sameness of person" to include "the notion of our living" both "in any two successive moments" and "now and hereafter", Butler suggests, what he elsewhere shows, that he is making the assumptions of the Platonic-Cartesian way. And, as we have already seen in Section 5 (v) of Chapter Eight, in this there are formidable and perhaps insurmountable difficulties.

The crux is to discover, or to develop, a viable concept of an incorporeal person; and that requires that we provide an account of the principles of identity and individuation which would apply to such incorporeal persons. Butler and the rest of the classical writers on personal identity all took it that our present concept of a person is of this kind. Granted this, and granted also that this present concept is coherent, then there will be no further problem of showing that and how a present (embodied) person could be said to be the same as a future (disembodied) person. If we reject this belief about the present concept, as I have maintained that we must, then the first problem is to find whether it is possible to develop a viable concept of incorporeal person. If and only if this can be done, then there will be a further problem of showing that and how future incorporeal persons could properly be said to be the same as particular present persons. In either case the most instructive way to begin is by studying the treatment of personal identity in Locke's *Essay*. It was, by the way, this treatment which provoked Butler's Dissertation.

2. *Locke's position*

Locke held that you cannot give an account of the meaning of 'same' in 'same this' or 'same that' without reference to the particular this or that involved: "It is not . . . unity of substance that comprehends all sorts of identity or will determine it in every case; but to conceive and judge of it aright, we must consider what idea the word it is applied to stands for" (II (xxvii) 8). So the first thing to consider in inquiring about personal identity—the meaning, that is, of the expression 'same person'—is the meaning of the word 'person'. Locke's definition is: "a thinking intelligent being, that has reason and reflection, and can consider itself as itself, the same thinking thing, in different times and places" (II (xxvii) 11). Such "a thinking intelligent being" clearly is, if not essentially incorporeal, at any rate not essentially corporeal. This Lockean idea of a person is distinguished from the idea of man, since "ingenious observation puts it past doubt" that "the idea in our minds, of which the sound 'man' in our mouths is the sign, is nothing else but of an animal of such a certain form" (II (xxvii) 9).

In his own words Locke's proposed solution to the problem of personal identity is: "That with which the consciousness of this present thinking thing *can* join itself, makes the same person, and is one self with it, and with nothing else; and so attributes to itself and owns all the actions of that thing, as its own, as far as that consciousness reaches, and no further; as everyone who reflects will perceive" (II (xxvii) 17: italics original).

The key word, 'consciousness', is troublesome. Locke does not employ it always in the same sense. Sometimes it seems to mean self-conscious, in the tricky and curious sense in which to say that someone is self-conscious is not to say that he is embarrassed: for instance, we read that "a being that . . . can consider itself as itself . . . does so only by that consciousness which is inseparable from thinking . . ." (II (xxvii) 11). Sometimes it seems to be more straightforwardly the consciousness which is the opposite of anaesthesia: for instance, when 'self' is defined as "a conscious thinking thing . . . which is sensible or conscious of pleasure or pain, capable of happiness or misery . . ." (II (xxvii) 17). But in his main statements of his position 'consciousness' is simply equivalent to 'memory', as can be seen from the words, "Could we suppose any spirit wholly stripped of all its memory or consciousness of past actions; as we find our minds always are of a great part of ours, and sometimes of them all . . ." (II (xxvii) 25).

Locke's position can, therefore, in modern terms be stated as follows: X at time two is the same person as Y at time one if and only if X and Y are both persons and X can remember at time two (his doing) what Y did, or felt or what have you at time one. The parenthetical '(his doing)' has to go in since, as Bernard Williams pointed out to me in his 'Personal Identity and Individuation', in the *Proceedings of the Aristotelian Society* for 1956–7, "we constantly say things like 'I remember my brother joining the army' without implying that I and my brother are the same person" (p. 233).

Having made this addition, and admission, it is worth stressing, as Williams does not, that all such utterances do still carry an implicit personal identity claim about the speaker—the claim that he was himself around and acquiring the information at the time in question. There is a necessary connection between memory and personal identity although, as we shall be seeing, not the one which Locke thought he had found. By making the insertion needed to meet Williams's point our reformulation becomes even more obviously exposed to "Butler's famous objection that memory, so far from constituting personal identity, presupposed it" (*ibid.*, p. 233). Yet this is not a fault in the reformulation, considered as a representation of Locke's position. For that position actually is wide open to that objection. I am at a loss to understand why Williams should, apparently, think that this reformulation is, as an interpretation of Locke, satisfactorily demolished by the Williams assertions: that it makes Locke's thesis "trivially tautologous [*sic*] and moreover lends colour to Butler's famous objection that memory, so far from constituting personal identity, presupposed it". Is it supposed to be obvious, or even true that Locke could not possibly be saying something which, in at least one of its meanings, is trivially tautological, and that Butler must be attacking his own factitious man of straw?

3. Objections to Locke's proposed solution
There are two lines of attack. Both are, I suggest, fatal to Locke's position. To understand what they are and why they must be thus fatal is of far more than merely antiquarian importance. For it seems that all those who want to give such an account of the identity of persons—an account, that is, of the identity of persons conceived as either essentially or potentially incorporeal—have to essay this attempt in one of two ways. Either, like Locke, they try to show that the identity of such persons is, or would be, somehow a matter of remembering or being able to remember. Or else they try to show, or perhaps more usually simply assume, that this identity is a matter of the identity of a supposed incorporeal substance. To understand that and why an account of personal identity in terms of memory cannot work is, therefore, to understand much more than that one proposal first published in the late 1600s is wrong.
(i) The first and simpler of the two lines of attack was taken by Butler in the third paragraph of the Dissertation from which I quoted in Section 1: ". . . though consciousness of what is past does . . . ascertain our personal identity to ourselves, yet to say, that it makes personal identity, or is necessary to our being the same persons . . ." is a "wonderful mistake". For "one should really think it self-evident, that consciousness of personal identity presupposes, and therefore cannot constitute, personal identity; any more than knowledge, in any other case, can constitute truth, which it presupposes".
There is little, if anything, which can usefully be added to a refutation so terse, so elegant and so decisive. It just is absurd

to say that 'he is the same person as did the deed' means no more and no less than 'he can remember that he is the same person as did the deed'. The absurdity is usually slightly masked, since such expressions as 'I can remember doing' or 'I remember seeing' do not explicitly spell out the truth that what is remembered is that the speaker is the same person as did or saw whatever it was. But we have already had to make this explicit in our reformulation of Locke's definition into modern terms, since without the parenthetical '(his doing)' that definition would become disastrously over-comprehensive.

Nevertheless, although there is little scope for reinforcing Butler's decisive objection, it will be profitable to underline its importance by giving one contemporary example of failure to come to terms with what was thus so well and so briefly said. Consider, therefore, A. M. Quinton's article on 'The Soul', published in *The Journal of Philosophy* for 1962. Quinton there explores the possibility of constructing "an empirical concept of the soul, which, like Locke's, interprets it as a sequence of mental states logically distinct from the body". Locke, he says, "clearly believed in the soul as the connected sequence of a person's conscious states, regarded this sequence as what a person essentially was, and held it to be capable of existing independently of the body". But on this view, Quinton urges, "the soul must . . . be a series of mental states that is identified through time in virtue of the properties and relations of these mental states themselves". He comments, very truly: "To establish the possibility of such a mental criterion of identity will be the hardest part of the undertaking" (p. 397).

Quinton begins that "hardest part" with an unwisely, but in this paper characteristically, offhand reference to the classical literature: "Locke's criterion of memory has been much criticised, and it is certainly untenable in some of the interpretations it has been given." Quinton in fact notices only part of one of the two classical objections, the one which we shall be considering in the next subsection: "It will not do to say that two mental states belong to the same soul if and only if whoever has the later one can recollect the earlier one, if the possibility of recollection involved is factual and not formal. For people forget things. . . ." (pp. 397–398).

Having thus accepted that he must speak only of what people could in principle remember and not of the much less which they can in fact recall, Quinton straightway proceeds to offer his own "more plausible criterion". This is "in terms of continuity of character and memory". The specification is formidably elaborate:

> Two soul-phases belong to the same soul, on this view, if they are connected by a continuous character and memory path. A soul-phase is a set of contemporaneous mental states belonging to the same momentary consciousness. Two soul-phases are directly continuous if they are temporally juxtaposed, if the character revealed by the constituents of each is closely similar, and if the later contains recollections of some elements of the earlier. Two soul-phases are indirectly continuous and connected by a continuous character and memory path if there is a series of soul-phases all of whose members are directly continuous with their immediate predecessors and successors in the series and if the original soul-phases are the two end points of the series (p. 398).

There is, you will surely be glad to hear, no call to labour to master the fine detail of this allegedly "more plausible criterion". For, under the impact of Butler's objection, Quinton's whole elaborate structure collapses just as quickly and just as completely as does Locke's more primitive and simple statement. It is quite clearly essential to this structure that both directly and indirectly continuous soul-phases should be linked—directly and indirectly, respectively—by recollections. Later soul-phases, in order to qualify for membership in the same soul, have to contain "recollections of some elements of the earlier" soul-phases. Now what is this if it is not attempting to define the identity of the soul in terms of the formal if not the factual possibility of remembering?

Nor can Quinton be defended by developing some suggestion that his "more plausible criterion" involves memory only in some thin or Pickwickian sense. That this is not so can be seen by rereading the last paragraph but two and the last paragraph but one. But, if a clincher is needed, consider how, in trying to meet the difficulty that the Quinton criterion might sometimes make 'identical' twins not merely, what in fact they often are, excessively similar, but even, as they cannot be, actually identical, Quinton raises the question: "Won't the later phases of one of the twins be as continuous in respect of character and memory with the earlier phases of the other as they are with his own earlier phases?" His answer is: "The environment of the two will be inevitably asymmetrical, each will at various times be nearer something than the other, each will block some things from the other's field of vision or touch; so there will always be some, perhaps trivial, difference in the memories of the two" (pp. 404–405). If Quinton is not appealing here, as he surely is, to the differences in what each twin in principle and in the full sense could remember, then his criterion must make the difference between the two depend on the actual precision and completeness of their memories. But this would entail the wildly paradoxical consequence that a pair of 'identical' twins not endowed with adequately full and precise powers of memory must really be identical and not a pair.

Notice, too, by the way, that Quinton's indirect but essential reference to the always and necessarily different spatial positions of his two twins must prejudice his expressed aim to develop "a mental criterion of identity". Incorporeal objects presumably have no position at all; and, even if they do, the positions of two different incorporeal objects will not always and necessarily be different.

(ii) The second line of attack on Locke's position demands very careful generalship. The crux is that Locke's criterion is at the same time both too strict in blackballing and too lenient in admitting candidates. Often his definition would not allow us to apply the expression 'same person', where we certainly should think it properly applicable; whereas in other cases Locke's ruling would be that it did apply, when we should certainly judge it not correctly applicable.

Before developing this second offensive, two distinctions have to be made. Two of the terms in Locke's definition are relevantly ambiguous. 'Can' may be: either 'can' as a matter of fact, hereafter rendered as 'can (factual)'; or it may be 'can' without self-contradiction be said to, hereafter rendered as 'can (logical)'. There is also a more subtle ambiguity in 'remember'. This is best brought out by symbolic examples. 'He knows p' entails p is true, whereas 'He said that he knew p, and he was not lying' does not entail p is true. Similarly, 'He remembers p' entails p is true; whereas 'He said that he remembered p, and he was not lying' does not entail p is true. For, just as it is both possible and common to be honestly mistaken in a claim to know something, so it is possible and common to be honestly mistaken in making a claim to remember something. When someone challenges a knowledge claim or a memory claim he is not necessarily, or even usually, challenging the claimant's integrity. He is much more likely to be questioning the truth of the proposition said to be known or remembered. If the proposition is in fact false, then this is sufficient to defeat the claim really to know or truly to remember. (Another possibility, mentioned only to be dismissed as here irrelevant, is that the critic is either challenging the adequacy of the grounds available to support the knowledge claim or challenging the implicit claim to have been in the past in a position which qualifies the claimant to be remembering now.) We have, therefore, to distinguish between genuine remembering, which necessarily involves the truth of the proposition said to be remembered, and making honest memory claims, which does not.

Let us now ring the changes on these alternative interpretations of 'can' and 'remember'.

(a) First, taking 'can' as logical and 'remember' as entailing the truth of what is remembered, Locke's definition could be made into a necessary truth, albeit a futile necessary truth. For it is manifestly true, though not a helpful definition of 'same person', that X at time two is the same person as Y at time one if and only if X and Y are both persons and X can (logically) remember at time two (his doing) what Y did, or what have you, at time one. It is manifestly true, since for it to be genuine memory the person remembering must necessarily be the same person as the person whose experience or activity he claims to be remembering as his own. On this interpretation, what we have is of course not open to attack on the ground that it is too exclusive or too inclusive. It is, simply, an otiose only too true truism.

(b) Second, taking 'remember' in the same way as referring to genuine remembering and 'can' as can (factual), Locke's definition is open to two objections. First, it excludes too much. Often, and rightly, we want to say that we must have done something or other, although we cannot for the life of us remember doing it. We are even prepared to accept full responsibility for such forgotten actions, at any rate provided that they are not too important. Even if they are important, and even if we want to disown or diminish our moral or legal responsibility for them, we are prepared to concede that we are the same persons as did them, unless, mistakenly, we think that personal identity is not merely the necessary but also the sufficient condition of full moral and legal responsibility.

The second objection to the second interpretation is the famous paradox, The Case of the Gallant Officer. This objection seems to have been made first by George Berkeley, but in a monochrome version, in *Alciphron* (VII 8). Later it was reproduced, in glorious Technicolor, in *Essays on the Intellectual Powers of Man* by Thomas Reid: "Suppose a brave officer to have been flogged when a boy at school, for robbing an orchard, to have taken a standard from the enemy in his first campaign, and also to have been made a general in advanced life" (III 6). Then, if the young officer could remember the flogging, and the general could remember taking the standard but not being flogged as a boy, on Locke's principles we should have to say that the general both is and is not the same person as the orchard robber. He is not the same, because he cannot now remember the robbery, and yet he is the same, because he is the same as the young officer who was in turn the same as the boy thief.

(c) The third possibility is to take 'can' as can (logical) and 'remember' as involving only the making of an honest memory claim. The objection to this is that it will let too much in. This point, too, was, it seems, first made by Berkeley in the private *Philosophical Commentaries*: "Wherein consists identity of person? Not in actual consciousness; for then I'm not the same person I was this day twelvemonth, but while I think of what I then did. Not in potential; for then all persons may be the same, for aught we know. . . . Two sorts of potential consciousness— natural and preternatural. In the last section but one I mean the latter" (§§200–202). It is our present point which Berkeley is making since his preternatural potential consciousness is obviously equivalent to ability to remember, in the present interpretations of 'can' and 'remember'.

(d) The fourth possible combination, that of 'can' as can (factual) with 'remember' as involving only the making of an honest memory claim, yields an interpretation open to all three objections made against the thesis in interpretations two and three. First, it leaves too much out, ignoring amnesia. Second, it lets too much in, ignoring paramnesia. Third it is internally inconsistent, being exposed to the paradox of The Case of the Gallant Officer.

Since more people are familiar with amnesia than with paramnesia, it is just worth remarking that paramnesia is not just a logical possibility but a real phenomenon. The stock and pathetic example is the British King George IV, who in his declining and demented years 'remembered' his dashing leadership at the Battle of Waterloo; notwithstanding that only a devoutly Lockean courtier, or an unscrupulous flatterer, could have pretended that the King must therefore have been present on that decisive field. Vulgar cases are provided daily by those who press forward, sincerely but without factual foundation, to claim the discredit for committing the latest newsy murder.

(iii) This completes the direct case against Locke's proposed solution of the main philosophical problem. But here, as in the political trials of less happier lands, the direct case can be rounded off with a sort of confession. For despite his insistence that, "the same consciousness being preserved, whether in the same or different substances, the personal identity is preserved", Locke is nevertheless, very reasonably but quite inconsistently, anxious lest "one intellectual substance may not have represented to it, as done by itself, what *it* never did, and was perhaps done by some other agent . . ." (II (xxvii) 13: italics original). Locke's anxiety is indeed sympathetic, and, as F. H. Bradley said in a slightly different connection: "It may help us to perceive, what was evident before, that a self is not thought to be the same because of bare memory, but only so when the memory is considered not to be defective" (Bradley, p. 85).

Nevertheless this sympathetic anxiety is wholly inconsistent with Locke's official account of personal identity; which requires him to deny that there can (logical) be honest but falsidical memory claims. If the phrase, 'being the same person as did that', is equivalent to the phrase, 'being a person able to remember (his) doing, or being able to be conscious of (his) doing, that', then you cannot consistently say that a person may both be able to remember doing, and yet not actually have done, some particular thing. Or, rather, to be absolutely strict, this can be made consistent only by interpreting 'remember' to refer exclusively to genuine veridical memory. But this move would again reduce this whole account of personal identity to vacuity.

In his desperation Locke falls on his knees:

> And that it never is so, will by us, till we have clearer views of the nature of thinking substances, be best resolved in the goodness of God; who as far as the happiness or misery of any of his sensible creatures is concerned will not, by a fatal error of theirs, transfer from one to another that consciousness which draws reward or punishment with it (II (xxvii) 13).

The Divine assistance for which Locke supplicates is beyond the resources even of Omnipotence. For on Locke's view there could be no sense in his own fear that people might lose or escape their deserts because they remembered doing what they had not in fact done. If anyone can remember doing something, then necessarily, according to Locke's account, he is in fact the same person as did that deed. Locke by making this desperate appeal tacitly confesses the inadequacy of his own account of personal identity. He also provides one more example of a phenomenon already all too familiar to the student of religious apologetic—the hope that the sheer physical power of a postulated God can make contradictions consistent and utterances to which no sense has been given sensible.

4. Job specification for a spiritual substance

Locke often speaks of "spiritual substances", and the like, with hesitation and perplexity. Yet he always takes it as given that a person as "a thinking intelligent being" is both essentially incorporeal and, in another and less perplexing sense, a substance. In this technical but clear interpretation a substance is defined as whatever can significantly be said to exist separately and in its own right. Much of Lewis Carroll's nonsense is produced by treating such things as grins and tempers, which are obviously not thus substances, as if they were like such things as faces and bones, which equally obviously are (Flew (4) IV 3 and passim; and compare subsections 5 (ii) and 5 (v) of Chapter Eight).

To see where Locke makes, and has to make, this assumption is a good way to come to realise what work incorporeal substances are conjured to do.

(i) First, it is only on the assumption that we, or our souls, are such substances that it can even make sense to suggest that we, or our souls, might exist before conception, or survive the dissolution of our bodies, or transmigrate from one body to another. Locke, however, is all the time entertaining these suggestions: "Should the soul of a prince", the *Essay* urges, "enter and inform the body of a cobbler . . . everyone sees he would be the same person as the prince" (II (xxvii) 15). It was because Plato was fully seized of this first point that in *Phaedo* Socrates labours to refute the suggestion that the soul might be a harmony of bodily elements. A harmony could not significantly be said to survive the dissolution of its elements (§§85D–86D and 91E–94E). Again, to take an illustration from this century, suppose that, like the author of *The Physical Basis of Personality*, we adopt as our motto the definition of 'personality' from the *Oxford English Dictionary*: "That quality or assemblage of qualities which makes a person what he is as distinct from other persons". Then it will not even make sense to speak, as that author later does, of "the relation of personality to the body we inherit" (Mottram, pp. 4 and 115).

(ii) Second, if you are trying to develop a notion of incorporeal person, or if you take it that persons in the present sense are not essentially corporeal; then, if your persons are not to become either awkwardly restless or embarrassingly ephemeral, you will need to assume that they are incorporeal substances. Consider Locke's dry, commonsensical objection to what he sees as a flight of French fancy:

> I grant that the soul, in a waking man, is never without thought, because it is a condition of being awake. But whether sleeping without dreaming be not an affection of the whole man, mind as well as body, may be worth a waking man's consideration; it being hard to conceive that anything should think and not be conscious of it (II (i) 11).

It is indeed hard, since Locke is here accepting from Descartes his official stipulative redefinition of the word 'think'; which is thus construed as comprising all and only modes of consciousness. Yet Descartes also insisted that people, or their souls, are in the present sense immaterial, spiritual substances. He maintained, furthermore, that thought—always in that official Cartesian sense—is the essential defining characteristic of such putative substances. So he left himself wide open to Locke's killing blow: ". . . methinks, every drowsy nod shakes their doctrine who teach that the soul is always thinking" (II (i) 13).

The moral for us is that, if people are incorporeal, and unless they are incorporeal substances endowed with some defining characteristic other than consciousness, then they must if ever they are neither awake nor dreaming simply go out of existence.

We have here a good sample of the profit to be gained from studying the philosophical classics. Quinton, in the article cited earlier, adopts a rather insouciant attitude towards all predecessors. Perhaps in consequence, he overlooks this second function of these postulated substances. He writes:

> Two soul-phases belong to the same soul . . . if they are connected by a continuous character and memory path. . . . Two soul-phases are directly continuous if they are temporally juxtaposed. . . . Two soul-phases are indirectly continuous . . . if there is a series of soul-phases all of whose members are directly continuous with their immediate predecessors and successors in the series and if the original soul-phases are the two end points of the series (p. 398).

By this criterion an earlier and a later soul-phase of what would ordinarily be called the same person will not belong to the same soul if that person happens in the meantime to have enjoyed a spell of dreamless sleep. Each one of us will have, or be, one more soul than we have had periods of total unconsciousness. It is fortunate for Quinton that Locke is no longer available to comment!

Another odd fault of Quinton's criterion, as he himself states it, is that it insists on actual recollections rather than on possibly unexercised capacities to recollect. Thus Quinton says: "Two soul-phases are directly continuous if they are temporally juxtaposed, if the character revealed by the constituents of each is closely similar, *and if the later contains recollections of some elements of the earlier*" (p. 398: italics supplied).

Since he goes on at once to define indirect continuity in terms of
direct continuity, and since his whole account of the identity of
a soul (or person) is in terms of direct and indirect continuity, it
appears that by his criterion a period of consciousness in which
one happened not to be actually exercising one's memory would
be as disruptive of one's continuous identity as a spell of
dreamless sleep. It is again instructive to compare Locke:

> That with which the consciousness of this present thinking thing
> *can* join itself, makes the same person and is one self with it, and
> with nothing else; and so attributes to itself and owns all actions
> of that thing, as its own, as far as that consciousness reaches, and
> no further; as everyone who reflects will perceive (II (xxvii) 17:
> italics original).

(iii) Third, as I argued against Hume in Section 5(v) of
Chapter Eight and in support of Price in Section 1 of Chapter
Nine, it makes no sense to speak of experiences save as the
experiences of some subject; and any such subject has to be in
the present sense a substance. This is not a point which Locke
spells out, since no one before Hume thought to challenge it.

Quinton devotes several pages to "the view that in each
person there is to be found a spiritual substance which is the
subject of his mental states and the bearer of his personal
identity". First he argues "that the existence of a spiritual
substance is logically distinct from its being the criterion of
personal identity"; and deploys "three strong, and indeed
fatal, arguments against the substance theory of personal
identity" (p. 393). Next he proceeds to the proposition "that
every mental state must have an owner", a proposition which
"has seemed self-evident to many philosophers" (p. 395). And
not only every mental state, one might add. Quinton concludes: "The strength of the argument lies in the fact that we
can assert the existence of some mental state, a feeling of anger
let us say, only when we are in a position to assert that we
ourselves are angry or that someone else is" (p. 396).

So far, perhaps, so good. But Quinton now goes on:

> It could be argued that it is a loose way of referring to the related
> series of other mental states or to the body or both with which any
> given mental state is universally associated by our manner of
> reporting such states. If it is something distinct from both of these,

as it has traditionally been believed to be, it is not properly to be
called the soul. . . . Its existence . . . is irrelevant to the problem
of the soul, which is that of whether a person is essentially mental
in character and so distinct from his body, a connected sequence
of mental states and not a physical object (p. 396).

These remarks betray misunderstanding of the classical
literature, and consequent failure to appreciate the problems.
For, as we have just seen, among the other tasks of the soul as a
spiritual substance are: both to provide continuity over the gaps
in consciousness; and to ensure that the soul is the sort of thing
which could significantly be said to survive by itself.

5. But how or what could such spiritual substances be?

If you will allow that a person is a (very special sort of) physical
object, that person-words all refer in sometimes different but
always essential ways to such familiar corporeal things; then, as
I argued in Chapter Eight, you will find it impossibly difficult
to maintain that people do or could survive physical dissolution.
But in that case you will have no great problem about preserv-
ing personal identity over the gaps in our consciousness, nor
about providing a subject for our mental states and other
characteristics. If, on the other hand, you want to be able to say
that people could in principle survive such dissolution, then it
seems as if you will have to maintain that a person is not only
incorporeal but also in the present sense, a substance. You will
need to maintain this, as we have just seen in Section 4, for
three different good reasons, deriving from the three different
functions there specified.

(i) Quinton fully appreciates that the idea of spiritual
substance has been thought to fulfil the third of these; although
his description of "the subject in this rather thin and formal
sense" suggests that he cherishes no great regard for either the
function or for the functionary. But he does not see the second,
arising from the fact that gaps in consciousness must constitute a
special problem for any incorporeal account of persons. He even
misses the first. After mentioning two other alternatives he
seems for a moment to become aware that something has been
overlooked. But Quinton has his own way of dealing with
predecessors:

K

If it is something distinct from both of these, *as it has traditionally been believed to be*, it is not properly to be called the problem of the soul, which is that of whether a person is essentially mental in character and so distinct from his body, a connected sequence of mental states and not a physical object (p. 393: italics supplied).

It is perhaps just worthwhile to devote the rest of the present subsection to a parenthetical correction of some important historical errors in the first paragraph of Quinton's article:

In the history of philosophy the soul has been used for two distinct purposes: first, as an explanation of the vitality that distinguishes human beings, and also animals and plants, from the broad mass of material objects; and, secondly, as the seat of consciousness. The first of these, which sees the soul as an ethereal but nonetheless physical entity . . . need not detain us. The second . . . the soul of Plato and Descartes, deserves a closer examination than it now usually receives.

This will not do. Certainly Plato did not see "the soul as an ethereal but nonetheless physical entity": that view is a view which he ridicules in *Phaedo* (§77D). Yet it is quite wrong to suggest that Plato did not conceive of the soul as a principle of life, and hence possibly as some sort of "explanation of the vitality that distinguishes human beings . . . from the broad mass of material objects". For both in *Republic* (§§352D–354A) and in *Phaedo* (§105 C9–D2) this clearly is at least part of his conception of the soul: in both he fails to distinguish sufficiently between an idea of the soul as the principle of life and the concept of the soul as the true and essentially incorporeal person; in *Phaedo* this failure is crucial to the plausibility of his great set-piece argument for human immortality (§§100B–105E).

It is also equally wrong to attribute what is in fact a distinctively Cartesian emphasis on consciousness to Plato. It was Descartes who first, after concluding that he or his soul was essentially an incorporeal thing, a spiritual or thinking substance, proceeded to define 'thinking' in terms of all and only consciousness. Thus Descartes said in the third *Meditation*: "By the word 'thought' I understand all that of which we are conscious as operating in us." So it is to Descartes, not Plato, that we owe the modern problem of mind and matter, considered as the problem of the relation of consciousness to stuff.

(ii) It is one thing to show who wants a notion of incorporeal substance, and why. It is quite another to show that they can have what they want. The crux is that the adjective in the expression 'incorporeal substance' negates the identifying content of the noun. Nor is this an emptily verbal point, to be parried by some equally verbal manoeuvre. For any stipulation making it possible to identify such a substance must make it correspondingly possible to show that in fact nothing of the sort enters at conception or leaves at death. The unacceptable price of providing such identification is that it thereby becomes in principle possible to falsify the claim that these substances exist. And this in part is why, I think, many spokesmen would be inclined to dismiss anything identifiable as only an astral body, not the real thing. Which in turn is in part why in Section 3(i) of Chapter Eight I proposed to classify corporeal souls along with astral bodies.

In Section 5(v) of Chapter Eight I quoted Penelhum on incorporeal substance: it is something "of which no independent characterisation is forthcoming". Hobbes in Chapter V of *Leviathan* is less gentle: "And therefore if a man should talk to me of 'a round quadrangle'; or 'accidents of bread in cheese';[47] or 'immaterial substances'; . . . I should not say he was in error, but that his words were without meaning: that is to say, absurd."

CHAPTER 11

A Trinity of Temptations

Chapter Ten did two main things. First, it demonstrated the impossibility of developing an account of personal identity in terms of memory. Second, after indicating three ways in which any Platonic-Cartesian view of man requires a notion of an incorporeal substance, it gave reason why this requirement cannot be met. The ill-starred attempt to develop such an account of personal identity is perennially tempting. It is tempting, first, because, if you are going to insist that people are, or might be, incorporeal; then there appears to be no more promising alternative way to try to go. But it is also tempting, second, because it is so easy to confound *how* we know with *what* we know.

Locke himself, for instance, was supposed to be investigating what we know when we know that this here now is the same person as did that there then. Yet Locke often instead answers the question how a fact of this kind might be known. Thus he tells us that on the "Great Day" of the Last Judgement everyone will "receive his doom, his conscience accusing or excusing him"; and again that, if he could remember "Noah's flood" as clearly as last winter's "overflowing of the Thames", then he could no more doubt "that he was the same self" who saw both floods (II (xxvii) 22 and 16). But, as Thomas Reid said, "in this doctrine not only is consciousness confounded with memory but, which is still more strange, personal identity is confounded with the evidence which we have of our personal identity" (Reid, III 6).

We can perhaps also distinguish two kinds of reason why it is tempting to argue, or assume, that people are, or might be, incorporeal substances. The first is that it may well seem that it is only upon this assumption that a way might be found over or around what, in Section 1 of Chapter Eight, I called "the enormous initial obstacle" to doctrines of personal survival and personal immortality. The second is that there are many features of our language and of our experience which may easily be misconstrued as warranting this assumption. It would be an enormous task, well beyond the capacity of a single short book, to tackle all these—as I believe—misunderstandings. Already the whole of Chapter Nine has been taken up with only one. Nevertheless it is just worth making three brief suggestions now.

1. Out-of-the-body experiences

Many people have reported that, usually in the crisis period of a serious illness, they have for some time observed, or 'observed', themselves from a point of view, often a moving point of view, other than that occupied by their own eyes. They have seen, or 'seen', themselves lying asleep in their beds; and so on. These are indeed very odd and remarkable experiences. But the fact that they undoubtedly do occur, albeit rarely, is no more a reason for saying that the person having such experiences is at the time disembodied, than is the fact that we can all imagine ongoings distant in either time or place a reason for saying that, when we are engaged in these imaginings, we are actually then or there, rather than when and where we in fact are.

The case of out-of-the-body experiences can for present philosophical if not for psychological purposes be assimilated to that of imagination. For what is in dispute is not what experiences are had or what images are formed, but how these experiences and these images are properly to be described. So, just as the correct answer to the question, 'Where and when is the woman imagining she is Helen of Troy, being seduced by Paris?', is, 'Wherever she is when she is doing the imagining; maybe in Warrington on a wet Sunday!'; so the answer to the question, 'Where was the patient when he was having out of the body experiences?', is—just as dispiritingly—'In his bed, apparently unconscious'.

The case of Lord Nelson is similar, but not the same. He took the fact that he sometimes suffered twinges where the arm lost in battle should have been as evidence that there are, and we are, incorporeal souls. Since these twinges undoubtedly fell into

the category of bodily sensations, they surely constitute
evidence, if anything, for astral bodies rather than for incorporeal souls. But, waiving that point, suppose that Nelson, or
those other amputees known to Descartes in his soldier days,
had reported itches and throbs as felt not where their limbs
should have been but way out of the body—say on the other
side of the public bar. This would still be no justification for
holding that they themselves were on that other side, and not
wherever they in fact were. I may feel a sensation, just as I may
imagine something, as here or there or anywhere. But I myself
am wherever I am doing the feeling, or the imagining.

2. Minding talk of minds

In Section 5(ii) of Chapter Eight we noticed that English and
other languages have many idioms referring to the mind:
'Ethiopia's win in the marathon was a triumph of mind over
matter'; 'Maybe he is odious, but he does have a first-class
mind'; 'Our younger daughter has a mind of her own'; and so
on. It is ordinarily quite wrong, although to some apparently
very tempting to construe these idioms as referring to elusive
entities—maybe even incorporeal substances. That this interpretation is wrong can easily be shown by providing translations
into pedestrian equivalents: 'The Ethiopian showed tremen-
dous guts in winning the marathon'; 'Maybe he is odious, but
he does have the ability to do first-class work'; 'Our younger
daughter makes her own decisions'; and so on.

The besetting danger here is to think, because we so often
have the best of reasons to apply these idiomatic forms of words
in their ordinary pedestrian interpretations, that we are therefore entitled to claim to know that we have, or are, incorporeal
mental substances. The mistake parallels that indicated in
Section 5(ii) of Chapter Seven, by which the indisputable fact
that we are all for ever making choices is mistaken to be an
equally inexpugnable reason for believing in the reality of free
will (libertarian). Consider, for example, a statement by the
well-known parapsychologist J. B. Rhine:

> The nature of the mind, or psyche, is by definition psychology's
> subject of study, though. . . . Even the word 'mind' as used by the
> layman, meaning something different from the brain, is no longer

in good standing. The student, therefore, finds . . . in modern
psychology text-books and lectures . . . very little on the mind as
a distinct reality (Rhine (2), p. 9).

But in Rhine he finds plenty. For Rhine thinks he knows that
there are such, if not exactly incorporeal, at any rate non-
physical substances. He therefore represents his putative psi-
phenomena always as the activities or the results of the
activities of these substances, rather than of flesh and blood
people: in telepathy "the mind could go out through space and
bring back knowledge of events which the senses could not
possibly reveal or the reason infer"; while, about psycho-
kinesis, since "We knew that in normal mental life the
subjective mind did something to the objective brain", the
question was "can the mind directly move or influence the
movement of an independent object outside its own organism?"
(Rhine (2), pp. 26 and 216; and, for further discussion,
compare Flew (1), IX).

3. Any body or no body?

Much of the material in Chapter Ten has been recycled from an
article first published in *Philosophy* for 1951. Commenting in
that article on Locke's definition of 'person', I wrote, with the
swinging confidence of youth:

> We learn the word 'people', by being shown people, by meeting
> them and shaking hands with them. They may be intelligent or
> unintelligent, introspective or extraverted, black, white, red or
> brown, but what they cannot be is disembodied or in the shape of
> elephants. Locke's definition would make it a contingent truth
> about people that some or all of them are either embodied in, or
> are of, human form. But, in the ordinary use of the word 'people',
> we do actually meet people and shake hands with them; we do
> not meet only the fleshy houses in which they are living or the
> containers in which they are kept. Nor is it logically possible for
> cougars (or parrots!) to be people. It is in short a necessary truth
> that people are of human shapes and sizes; and, not a contingent
> fact that some or all people inhabit human bodies or are of human
> form (p. 59).

This claim was challenged by James Moulder in *Philosophy*
for 1973. He starts, as I did, from the observation that Locke
defines 'person' as "a thinking intelligent being, that has reason

and reflection, and can consider itself as itself, the same thinking thing, in different times and places" (II (xxvii) 11). Moulder also notices, as Locke did (*ibid.*, 9 and 10), that given this definition, and given "a very intelligent rational parrot" which could "discourse, reason, and philosophise"; then we should have to say that this parrot, though clearly not a member of the species homo sapiens was nevertheless a person. But whereas I took this to be an objection to Locke's definition, Moulder construes it as an indication that there could be persons in or of unambiguously non-human forms. Moulder then proceeds headlong to far more important conclusions:

> If . . . something qualifies as a person simply because it has a capacity for certain kinds of conscious states, then, surely, corporeal characteristics are not among the defining charac- teristics of a person. . . . And . . . then the question of whether or not there are non-corporeal or immaterial persons is, obviously, one which has to be answered not on apriori or semantic grounds but on de facto ones . . . then there seems to be no reason for refusing to admit that we are not essentially immaterial objects (p. 185).

(i) The first thing which has to be said here, and said very firmly and emphatically, is that this—as the rally drivers say—is going a bit quick. For the reasons indicated in the previous chapter, and for others too, it simply will not do to move immediately without further argument, from the contention that distinctively personal attributes can significantly be predicated not only of human beings but also of living organisms of other kinds, to the conclusions that it makes sense to talk of immaterial or incorporeal substances, and that some or all of these distinctively personal attributes can also be significantly predicated of such "not essentially material objects".

(ii) The second, much less important, question is whether any references to the human form are part of the present meaning of 'person' and other person words. The first mildly interesting thing to notice here is that Locke himself thought that the true answer was 'Yes'. For, at the end of his considera- tion of The Case of the Rational Parrot, he writes: "For I presume it is not the idea of a thinking or rational being alone that makes the idea of a man in most people's sense, but of a body, so and so shaped, joined to it"; and later, "I know that, in the ordinary way of speaking, the same person, and the same man stand for one and the same thing" (II (xxvii) 10 and 15).

Certainly, we must admit that, supposing parrots or dolphins or you name the species were to manifest a sufficient variety and consistency of quasi-personal initiative and response, then nearly everyone would be prepared to describe these still non-human beings as a kind of persons. But it would be a token of a very common type of mistake to interpret this admission as conceding that there is no essential reference to the human form in the present meaning of 'person' and other person words. The point is that the present meanings, and hence the implications, of our terms, are determined by their present correct usage. The facts, if they be facts, that we either ought to or actually would change our usage in ways which must shift the meanings and hence the implications of certain terms *granted such and such suppositions*; provide no good reason for concluding that the terms in question do in fact now, *when those suppositions are not in fact realised*, have those possible meanings, and carry those corresponding possible implications.

The only conclusion which we are entitled to draw from the concession made at the beginning of the previous paragraph is, rather, that, besides any presently essential reference to the specifically human form, the present concept of a person also makes essential reference to certain distinctive capacities for initiative and response. Whether or not it is necessary to be an organism of one particular kind, it is certainly not sufficient.

(iii) Moulder also refers to P. F. Strawson's basic contention "that the concept of a person is the concept of 'a type of entity such that *both* predicates ascribing states of consciousness *and* predicates ascribing corporeal characteristics . . . are equally applicable to a single individual of that single type' ''; and Moulder comments that this "suggests that he is conflating the concept of a human being, in the technical sense of [a member of the species—A.F.] homo sapiens, and the concept of a person" (p. 183: italics original).

First, it ought not to suggest so much; although it is significant that, to Moulder, it does. It ought not to suggest so much because, while the passage quoted within my quotation clearly

154 GOD, FREEDOM, AND IMMORTALITY

requires that persons be corporeal, it neither says nor suggests
that only an organism of one particular species can qualify.

Second, it is worth noticing, and regretting, the afterthought
seventh section which Strawson inserted into the revised
version of his 'Persons'. In this revised, but not improved,
version Strawson urges: "Each of us can quite intelligibly
conceive of his or her individual survival of bodily death. The
effort of imagination is not even great." He proceeds to draw
out two consequences: "that the strictly disembodied is strictly
solitary"; and "that in order to retain his idea of himself as an
individual, he must always think of himself as *dis*embodied, as a
former person" (Strawson (3), pp. 115 and 116: italics original;
none of this appears in Strawson (2)).

I have already had my own say in Chapters Nine and Ten,
both about this allegedly easy exercise of the imagination, and
about the intractable difficulties of what is presupposed by talk
of such disembodied individuals. I will here add only one point,
and that of a different kind. Whatever the truth about my
contentions, Strawson's afterthoughts on "*dis*embodied . . .
former persons" cannot be squared with his own basic proposition: that persons are tokens of "a type of entity such that *both*
predicates ascribing states of consciousness *and* predicates
ascribing corporeal characteristics . . . are equally applicable to
a single individual of that single type". Really to imagine myself
disembodied would have to be to imagine (the same person as)
me disembodied. Now, either we imagine a person or we do
not. But former persons, if they really are only former persons,
are no more a sort of person than ex-wives, if they really are
ex-wives, are a sort of wives. We cannot, therefore, allow
Strawson these manoeuvres: first, in his easy imaginings to
assume that his putative disembodied beings would be persons;
and then, when the going gets a bit rougher, to sidestep the
consequent charge of inconsistency by calling them *former*, and
hence not, persons.

CHAPTER 12

What Does it Mean to Ask: 'What is the Meaning of Life?'

1. Another kind of contention
In Chapter Five of Part One I examined an argument different in kind from those considered in Chapters Three and Four. Pascal's Wager offers a reason, motive, for self-persuasion rather than a reason, evidence, for the truth of what is proposed for belief. In this final chapter of Part Three we shall look at a contention which is like Pascal's Wager in that it does not really provide any evidence that the approved claims about God and immortality are true. But what it does do is rather different. It urges that the truth of these claims is presupposed by some desired and desirable way of life.

The most famous contentions of this particular sort are to be found in Kant's *Critique of Practical Reason*. For, although Kant always insists that there can be no demonstration of the existence of God, he nevertheless maintains that it is a matter not—as with Pascal—of prudence but of duty "that we should presuppose . . . the existence of God . . .; that is, it is morally necessary to assume the existence of God" (II (ii) 5). The same holds, Kant believes, of immortality also. But I propose now to examine a similar contention in an equally famous author, whose arguments are rarely appraised as arguments. The contention is that our lives can have meaning only on the assumptions of the existence of God and of human immortality. The author is Tolstoy, who wrote in *A Confession*: "What real result will come of my life?—Eternal torment or eternal bliss. What meaning has life that death does not destroy?—Union with the eternal God: heaven" (p. 50).

2. Tolstoy's argument

This autobiographical fragment marks one of the turning-points in Tolstoy's development. It was the first work of the period of his intensive study of the Gospels: the period which begins after the completion of *War and Peace* and *Anna Karenina,* and which continues until the return to fiction in *The Death of Ivan Ilyich* and *The Power of Darkness.*

(i) He begins by explaining that he was both baptised and raised in the Orthodox Christian faith. "But when I abandoned the second course at the University at the age of eighteen I no longer believed any of the things I had been taught" (p. 3). Tolstoy's loss of faith came about not as the result of any spiritual struggle but seemed to have been rather a recognition of the fact that he had never really had and lived by any real Christian conviction. In his late teens and for most of his twenties he lived the sort of life that was expected of an aristocrat of his country and period. Then he took up with literature: "faith in the meaning of poetry and in the develop-ment of life was a religion, and I was one of its priests" (p. 9). He recognised that his fellow professional writers were a poor lot. Nevertheless: "I naively imagined that I was a poet and artist and could teach everybody without myself knowing what I was teaching" (p. 10). Travel in Europe confirmed him in "the faith of striving after perfection" (p. 12). But in this period he suffered two traumata: he witnessed in Paris an execution by the guillotine; and his brother died young after a long and painful illness "not understanding why he had lived and still less why he had to die" (p. 13). Compare in *Anna Karenina* the impact on Constantine Levin of the death of his brother Nicholas (III (xxxi)).

Marriage swept all cosmic concerns out of Tolstoy's head, temporarily: "The new conditions of happy family life com-pletely diverted me from all search for the general meaning of life. . . . So another fifteen years passed. . . . But five years ago something very strange began to happen to me. At first I experienced moments of perplexity and arrest of life, as though I did not know what to do or how to live . . . these moments of perplexity began to recur oftener and oftener. . . . They were always expressed by the questions: What is it for? What does it lead to?" (pp. 14–15).

Tolstoy's phrasing is perhaps more apt here than he realised. For interpreted as requests for information the questions he was asking would be rather silly. It is better to construe them as expressions of "arrest of life" formulated in a way which is partly misleading.

He explains: "Before occupying myself with my Samara estate, the education of my son, or the writing of a book, I had to know *why* I was doing it" (p. 16: italics original). So far of course so good. It is perfectly reasonable to ask why you are doing what you are doing. But Tolstoy in this phase "of perplexity and arrest of life" would not take an answer for an answer. To all the replies which came into his mind he responded again: "What of it? What for?" He asks himself why he is making plans for the education of his son. The obvious reply is that he wants to do his best for the boy. Since this is both what he wants to do and what he ought to do it is hard to see what further or better reason there could be for doing what he is doing. As Hume put it: "It is impossible there can be progress in infinitum, and that one thing can always be a reason why another is desired. Something must be desirable on its own account, and because of its immediate accord or agreement with human sentiment and affection" (Hume (2), App. I). So to go on, as Tolstoy does, asking "What for?" after you have already seen how your contemplated course of action is rooted in your fundamental sentiments and affections might seem to be just silly, an indication of a failure to appreciate the scope and function of the question "What for?"

But, of course, in Tolstoy there is much more to it than that. The point is that all ordinary desires, affections, and satisfactions have lost their power and appeal: precisely this is that "arrest of life" of which the obsessively reiterated interrogatives are symptomatic. "I could find no reply at all. The questions would not wait, they had to be answered at once, and if I did not answer them it was impossible to live" (p. 17). Compare again *Anna Karenina*, and how "though he was a happy and healthy family man Levin was several times so near to suicide that he hid a cord he had lest he should hang himself, and he feared to carry a gun lest he should shoot himself" (VIII (ix)).

(ii) So far it has been suggested only that the interrogative forms here are partly misleading: for it is hard to see what answers, other than those of the kind already rejected, could be given to Tolstoy's symptomatic questionings straightforwardly construed. But they are not wholly misleading: for it is at least quite clearly a genuine question of what would remedy the pervasive disease of which they were expressions, of what would enable him to pick up again after this "arrest of life": "My life came to a standstill" (p. 17).

At the beginning of the following Section iv a fresh idea is introduced. It is that what makes Tolstoy's life meaningless, and what apparently should make all human life equally meaningless, is the (presumed) fact that every individual ends in "suffering and real death—complete annihilation" (p. 18). The passage runs: "My life came to a standstill . . . there were no wishes the fulfilment of which I could consider reasonable. . . . The truth was that life is meaningless. . . . It was impossible to . . . avoid seeing that there was nothing ahead but suffering and real death—complete annihilation" (pp. 17–18). As usual there are passages in the great novels where ideas of much the same sort had been expressed. Thus in *War and Peace* Pierre Bezukhov thinks to himself: "All such 'words of honour' are conventional things with no definite meaning, especially if one considers that tomorrow one may be dead. . . ." But there the author adds: "Pierre often indulged in reflections of this sort, nullifying all his decisions and intentions" (I (iii)).

But here, where Tolstoy is speaking in his own person, there is no similarly astringent comment. Here and now what began as clinical autobiography is developing pretensions to wider insight into the depths of the supposedly universal human situation. Tolstoy is sliding from the merely autobiographical: "there were no wishes the fulfilment of which I could consider reasonable"; to the ostensibly objective conclusion that suffering and mortality really must withdraw all reasonableness from every attempt to satisfy any ordinary human desire.

It is the notion of the meaninglessness of life which appears to provide the crucial middle term: if life is meaningless, then there can be no desires the fulfilment of which would be reasonable; but if there is nothing ahead but "suffering and real death", then life must be meaningless. Yet whatever plausibility this argument may have depends on interpreting this crucial middle term ambiguously: the basic sense for

Tolstoy is that in which to say that life is meaningless is to say that there are no human desires the fulfilment of which would be reasonable. But sometimes, as in the present argument, the expression is also so construed as in effect simply to mean that life does end in "suffering and real death".

There is a price to be paid even for an unequivocal interpretation of "the meaninglessness of life" as equivalent to "the fact that all our lives end in suffering and real death". If we give the words this meaning then any attempt to press the question, 'What is the meaning of life?', must amount to a prejudicial insistence that after all we do not really suffer and die—or, at any rate, not finally. Similarly, to lament the meaninglessness of life will not be to lament something which may or may not be the tragic consequence of our mortality and passibility: it will be to express distress over just those very facts of the human condition. But the result of using the expression "the meaninglessness of life", as Tolstoy does, ambiguously, is to make it seem as if some reason had been given for taking it that the only truly deep and adequate response to the facts so labelled is a final decisive arrest of life by suicide. That is the conclusion of Section iv, although it is developed later in Section vii.

(iii) In Section v Tolstoy tells us how he proceeded to look for answers to his questions in the sciences, but unsuccessfully: "I sought in all the sciences, but far from finding what I wanted, became convinced that all who like myself had sought in knowledge for the meaning of life had found nothing" (p. 23). These questions are all, he thinks, fundamentally the same question, differently formulated. One, considered in 2(i), is: "Why should I live, why wish for anything, or do anything?" This, for reasons elucidated in 2(ii) is taken to be the same thing as asking: "Is there any meaning in my life that the inevitable death awaiting me does not destroy?" (p. 24). In Section vi, by way of Socrates and Schopenhauer, Tolstoy reaches *Ecclesiastes* and the story of the Buddha's discovery of disease, death, and decay. For all this, except the reference to the Buddha, compare again the spiritual struggles of Levin in *Anna Karenina* (VIII, viii and ix).

In Section vii Tolstoy lists what he regards as the only four possible reactions to this supposed fact of the meaninglessness of life. The first, ignorance, is only for the naïvely innocent: it consists in "not understanding that life is an evil and an absurdity". This is out: "One cannot cease to know what one does know" (p. 39). The second, called 'epicureanism', is substantially that of the author of *Ecclesiastes*. Although "That is the way in which the majority of people of our circle make life possible for themselves", such epicureanism can, in Tolstoy's view, result only from shallowness and lack of imagination. This, again, is out: "I could not imitate these people; not having their dullness of imagination I could not artificially produce it in myself" (p. 40). The third option "is that of strength and energy". This consists in suicide: "I saw that this was the worthiest way of escape and I wished to adopt it" (p. 41). "The fourth way is that of weakness. It consists in seeing the truth of the situation and yet clinging to life, knowing that nothing will come of it" (p. 41). This was Tolstoy's own first response, as well as that of Pierre Bezukhov and Constantine Levin.

If these were merely the musings of some character in a novel they might perhaps be allowed to pass. Though even here it is as worthwhile as it is unfashionable to emphasise that if the novel or indeed creative literature generally is to be anything more than a pastime, then men of letters must be prepared for a criticism of content which presses beyond all purely literary and dramatic considerations. Certainly, presented as they are, as in part some contribution to our thinking about the problems of world outlook, Tolstoy's ideas categorically must be challenged. It just will not do at all to offer the facts, or supposed facts, of "suffering and real death" as if they must be, or would have to be, taken as compulsive reasons for deciding "that life is an evil and an absurdity". The fact that all lives contain evils gives no ground sufficient for inferring that all or even any lives are wholly or even predominantly evil. The fact that no life lives for ever does not necessarily devalue all the possible activities and achievements of a lifetime.

Apparently Tolstoy was one of those inclined to hold, as if this were a necessary truth, that nothing can matter unless it goes on forever; or, at any rate, eventually leads to something else which does. But there really is nothing at all ineluctable, or even especially profound, about this particular value commitment. It is at least no less rational to hold that it is precisely our mortality which makes what we do, or fail to do, so overwhelmingly important. And there is not the slightest warrant for suggesting that this alternative and opposite reaction is possible only for those who are lacking in imagination. Consider the words of another character in another novel: "You don't realise how much more noble it is, how much more tragic and yet exhilarating . . . to have a life ephemeral but infinitely precious, precious *because* it is the only life we have".[48]

(iv) "Life is a senseless evil, that is certain, said I to myself" (p. 42). Just when he thinks this unsatisfactory conclusion satisfactorily established Tolstoy is struck by a paradoxical observation: "The reasoning showing the vanity of life is not so difficult, and has long been familiar to the very simplest folk; yet they have lived and still live. How is it that they all live and never think of doubting the reasonableness of life?" (p. 43). It is, apparently, because they know the contrary: "From the most distant times . . . people have lived knowing the argument about the vanity of life, which has shown me its senselessness, and yet they lived attributing some meaning to it" (p. 44).

This is a turning-point, both of Tolstoy's personal story and of the development of his argument. It is here that he begins to find what he is prepared to call the meaning of life. To appreciate the logic, or the lack of logic, of what is going on, it is essential to bear clearly in mind the various distinctions already drawn. It is one thing to ask what would in fact relieve Tolstoy's Disease, the "arrest of life" considered simply as a paralysing psychological condition. It is quite another to inquire what sense, if any, has been given in this particular and peculiar context to the interrogative sentences the utterance of which is symptomatic of that distressing psychological condition.

Again, we must distinguish between the facts of suffering and universal mortality which sometimes are taken as being, and sometimes as showing, the senselessness of life, and these evaluative conclusions—about the unreasonableness and the pointlessness of it all—which are sometimes supposed to follow from, and are sometimes equated with, those supposed facts. Certainly, as a matter of biography, the idea of "suffering and real death" presented itself to Tolstoy as if it must involve a devaluation of all values. But, as we have seen, there is no general necessity about this at all, whether logical or psychological. Nor is there anything uniquely deep or dignified about the approved suicidal response to these fundamental facts of the human condition.

What at this point struck Tolstoy so forcibly becomes para- doxical only when you take it, as he apparently does, that these simple people must somehow know something which has completely eluded his inquiry. This assumption can be seen in his saying that "there is a whole humanity that lived and lives as if it understood the meaning of its life, *for without understanding it it could not live*" (p. 43; italics mine).

Now, of course, it clearly is true that these people have, in a sense, got something that Tolstoy then had not: for they are clearly not suffering from the condition which he so strikingly dubs "arrest of life". But, as we have seen, this condition is by no means a necessary response to, nor a necessary consequence of, a recognition of certain fundamental facts. He is, therefore, not warranted to assume that the absence of this pathological condition in the simplest folk, combined with the presence of a capacity to appreciate some trite reasonings, provides any sort of indication that they must possess knowledge of life's meaning, in the senses in which he has been employing that expression.

Simply by not suffering from arrests of life, and by being acquainted with such trite arguments, they do not show that they must possess some fount of secret knowledge—philo- sophical knowledge that and why his earlier reasonings are unsound, or metaphysical knowledge that after all we are not really mortal, or that suffering is somehow not what it seems. Nevertheless, Tolstoy was not altogether wrong in thinking that there was something to be learnt from the mere existence of such simple folk, unworried by his tormenting sense of cosmic futility. It might, for instance, lead one to suspect that there are flaws in his questions and in his arguments, which there are. It might also suggest that he could learn from these unsophisti- cated examples at least one way to escape from his psychological condition, as in fact he did. What we surely need here is Ryle's distinction between knowing *how* and knowing *that*; the peasants may indeed know how to live their lives free of all sophisticated psychological disabilities, but this by no means presupposes the possession of any theoretical knowledge not vouchsafed to their unfortunate social superiors.[49]

(v) In Section viii Tolstoy tells how an independent force came to the rescue in his dissatisfactions: "Something else was also working which I can only call a consciousness of life." This force dragged Tolstoy's attention away from "that narrow circle of rich learned, and leisured people to which I belonged" and towards "the whole life of mankind that surrounded me on all sides" (p. 45). But he does not now want merely to break down what he has come to regard as his unhealthy isolation from the life of ordinary people. He begins to develop a mystique of the masses: "Rational knowledge, presented by the learned and wise, denies the meaning of life, but the enormous masses of men, the whole of mankind, receive that meaning in irrational knowledge. And that irrational knowledge is faith" (p. 47). This mystique later betrays him into some memorably unpersuasive utterances: "All that people sincerely believe in must be true; it may be differently expressed but it cannot be a lie, and therefore if it presents itself to me as a lie, that only means I have not understood it" (p. 68). It would surely be hard to find, even in the prophetic writings of D. H. Lawrence, anything more egregiously grotesque.

Yet Tolstoy was no wilful irrationalist. He was tormented by this apparent contradiction between the deliverances of reason and of faith: "By faith it appears that in order to understand the meaning of life I must renounce my reason, the very thing for which alone a meaning is required" (p. 47).

He begins in Section ix to explore as a possible way to the resolution of his antinomy the idea that "rational knowledge" deals only with the finite, whereas "irrational knowledge" is always concerned with a relation between the finite and the infinite. But, like others who have tried to separate two exclusive spheres of influence, he finds difficulty both in determining appropriate territories and in maintaining the necessary barriers. At the end of Section ix, he writes: "I began to understand that in the replies given by faith is stored up the deepest human wisdom and that I had no right to deny them on the ground of reason, and that those answers are the only ones which reply to life's question" (p. 53).

Yet at the beginning of Section x Tolstoy, like everybody else,

finds himself confronted with rival faiths and rival interpretations; and he in fact resorts to some sort of rational criticism as
the only sensible method of attempting to decide between their
different claims. It is with an account of the first stages of this
process that the rest of *A Confession* is occupied; and in the whole
period of his life to which this forms a prologue Tolstoy devoted
himself to a strenuous, and radically protestant, study both of
the Gospels and of systematical theologies. The upshot was
something very far indeed from the uncritical and superstitious
faith of a muzhik.

However, we are here concerned with all this only in so far
as it bears on his argument about the meaing of life. For present
purposes what needs to be underlined once again is that the
peasants who seem able to teach Tolstoy a lesson in *how* to live
do not thereby and necessarily reveal any knowledge *that*
something is the case. There is, therefore, no call, at least on this
account, to search for some sphere of the infinite for such "irrational knowledge" to be about. Again, the secret of the peasants
is not knowledge *that* the finite and the infinite are thus and thus
arranged, but knowledge of *how* to go on living, and to allege
that they—along surely with the despised epicureans and
others—possess this sort of knowledge is in this case only another
way of saying that they all enjoy rude mental health.

Furthermore, and finally, even if it were to be established that
for some men, or for all men, to hold certain metaphysical
beliefs is a condition of full well-being, this suspiciously Jungian
fact would still have not the slightest tendency to show that any
such therapeutic beliefs are actually true. The antinomy, which
was at the end of Section viii tormenting Tolstoy, thus dis-
appears, not because "rational knowledge" and "irrational
knowledge" tell the truth about different spheres, but because
no sufficient reason has been provided for believing that the
latter tells any truth at all.

3. *Epilogue*

Earlier in *A Confession* there were hints of something different,
and better: "I sought in all the sciences, but far from finding
what I wanted, became convinced that all who like myself
had sought in knowledge for the meaning of life had found
nothing"; and now he confesses: "The solution of all the

possible questions of life could evidently not satisfy me" (pp. 23 and 48).

It is interesting to compare some characteristically oracular utterances of a philosopher whom we know to have been personally much influenced by the writings of Tolstoy. In the *Tractatus Logico-Philosophicus*, Wittgenstein proclaims:

> We feel that even if all possible scientific questions be answered, the problems of life have still not been touched at all. Of course there is then no question left, and just this is the answer. The solution of the problem of life is seen in the vanishing of this problem. (Is not this the reason why men to whom after long doubting the sense of life became clear, could not then say wherein this sense consisted?)

He then adds, in a vein still more apocalyptic: "There is indeed the inexpressible. This shows itself; it is the mystical" (6.52, 6.521, and 6.522).[50]

In her curiously hierophantic *Introduction*, G. E. M. Anscombe urges that Wittgenstein cannot be interpreted as saying only the negative thing which he seems to be saying in the first four of the six sentences quoted: quite rightly, for the two following sentences are used to insist that there is after all something to be said, albeit something which unfortunately happens to be unsayable. She goes on to write of Tolstoy, "whose explanations of what he thought he understood are miserable failures; but whose understanding is manifested, and whose preaching comes through, in a story like *Hadji Murad*" (Anscombe, p. 170).

In the light of the whole previous argument it becomes possible to see that and how this is both partly right and partly wrong.

It is right in its suggestion that what Tolstoy was seeking, and preaching, was primarily an attitude to life and a way of life; something combining dignity, realism, and peace of mind. It is wrong in assuming that such a way and such an attitude must be connected necessarily with some mystic truth: no good reason whatsoever has been given for believing that the peace of mind of Platon Karatayev, and that eventually achieved by Pierre Bezukhov, by Constantine Levin, or by Hadji Murad either validates or presupposes logically any propositions about some infinite shadow world outside the world.

Indeed what should strike the ideologically minded reader is that although Murad was a Hadji—one, that is, who has made the great pilgrimage to Mecca—his character is not in fact presented as formed by the doctrines of Islam. Again, in *War and Peace*, Pierre Bezukhov's "mental change" is not a conversion to a dogma—not even to an inexpressible dogma—but rather the acquisition of "that tranquillity of mind, that inner harmony, which had so impressed him in the soldiers at the battle of Borodino" (XIII (iii)). His new-found 'faith' is a faith wholly devoid of intellectual content, and the 'answers' which he now accepts are doctrinally as empty as the original symptomatic 'questions' (XV (v)). In *Anna Karenina*, similarly, Constantine Levin is not initiated into any truths necessary to salvation. Yet he too comes to feel that "my whole life, independently of anything that may happen to me, is in every moment no longer meaningless as it was before, but has an unquestionable meaning of goodness with which I have the power to invest it" (VIII (xix): compare x, xi and xiii).

The appreciation of this antithesis between the concern about a way of life and the discovery of mystic truth may provide a clue to a constructive understanding of Tolstoy's later religious teaching. We have seen how Tolstoy was "brought to acknowledge that all live humanity has another irrational knowledge— faith which makes it possible to live"; and this, at least in *A Confession*, he mistakes to be a knowledge that something is the case. But later, in such specifically religious works as the studies of the Gospels and *What I Believe*, this traditional doctrine seems to disappear; and the teaching is of a way of life, without benefit of any eschatological threats and promises. Indeed we seem to have there a religion which looks as if it really might be completely analysable without reference to any doctrinal content.

There have in recent years been many attempts by philosophers, both friendly and unfriendly to religion as they see it, to develop analyses of this kind. One of the most notorious was that offered by a Cambridge professor freshly baptised in King's College chapel. A religious assertion, he said, is "the assertion of an intention to carry out a certain behaviour policy, subsumable under a sufficiently general principle to be a moral one, together with the implicit or explicit statement, but not necessarily the assertion of certain stories". Perhaps the most interesting aspect of this suggestion lies in its emphatic recognition that stories which are not even believed to be literally true may nevertheless have an enormous influence: "Next to the Bible and the Prayer Book the most influential work in English Christian religious life has been a book whose stories are frankly recognised as fictitious—Bunyan's *Pilgrim's Progress*; and some of the most influential works in setting the moral tone of my generation were the novels of Dostoevsky" (Braithwaite, pp. 32 and 27).

Now to proffer anything so lacking in doctrinal content as a descriptive analysis of the religion of the Saints and of the Fathers, of the Popes and of the Reformers, would be—or, should I say, was?—absurd. But, if we are considering only Tolstoy's own idiosyncratic final reading of Christianity, then it is at least not obviously and immediately out of the question to attempt an analysis in these terms, or in some variation on or combination of them. And to the extent that this is possible his final goal becomes altogether appropriate to the urge which originally drove him on his religious quest. That quest arose from an intolerable dissatisfaction with his condition. Certainly that "arrest of life" expressed itself in interrogatives. But, as we have seen, these are most charitably to be regarded not as questions requiring an answer but as symptomatic utterances.

NOTES

1. This and some later translations from the Latin are mine.
2. See Chapter VI of Lewis Carroll's *Through the Looking Glass:*

> "But 'glory' doesn't mean 'a nice knock-down argument' ", Alice objected.
> "When I use a word", Humpty Dumpty said in rather a scornful tone, "it means just what I choose it to mean—neither more nor less."
> "The question is", said Alice, "whether you *can* make words mean so many different things."
> "The question is", said Humpty Dumpty, "which is to be master—that's all."

3. See the paper 'Presumptions' by my former colleague Patrick Day in the *Proceedings of the XIVth International Congress of Philosophy* (Vienna, 1968), Vol V, at p. 140. I am pleased that it was I who first suggested to him an exploration of this unfrequented philosophical territory.
4. The whole passage, in which Aquinas gives his reasons for believing that the Christian candidate does, and that of Muhammad does not, constitute an authentic revelation of God should be compared with some defence of the now widely popular assumption that the contents of a religious faith must be without evidential warrant.

   A. C. MacIntyre, for instance, while he was still himself a Christian, argued with great vigour for the Barthian thesis that "Belief cannot argue with unbelief: it can only preach to it". Thus he urged: ". . . suppose religion could be provided with a method of proof . . . since the Christian faith sees true religion only in a free decision made in faith and love, the religion would by this vindication be destroyed. For all possibility of free choice would have been done away. Any objective justification of belief would have the same effect . . . faith too would have been eliminated" (MacIntyre, p. 209).

   Now, first, in so far as this account is correct any commitment to a system of religious belief has to be made altogether without evidencing reasons. MacIntyre himself concludes with a quotation from John Donne to illustrate the "confessional voice" of faith, commenting: "The man who speaks like this is beyond argument" (MacIntyre, p. 211). But this, we must insist, would be nothing to be proud of. It is certainly no compliment, even if it were a faithful representation, to portray the true believer as necessarily irrational and a bigot.

   Furthermore, second, it is not the case that where sufficient evidence is available there can be no room for choice. Men can, and constantly

M

do, choose to deceive themselves about the most well-evidenced, inconvenient truths. Also no recognition of any facts, however clear, is by itself sufficient to guarantee one allegiance and to preclude its opposite. MacIntyre needs to extend his reading of the Christian poets to the greatest of them all. For the hero of Milton's *Paradise Lost* had the most enviably full and direct knowledge of God. Yet Lucifer, if any creature could, chose freely to rebel.

5. For a thorough treatment of the questions of Hume interpretation see Chapter VIII of Flew (2), and for a more general treatment of the actual theoretical issues themselves see my article 'Miracles' in *The Encyclopaedia of Philosophy*, edited by Paul Edwards.

6. I copied this from a review in the *New Zealand Rationalist*. But I confess that I failed to make any record either of the issue in which it appeared or of the work under review; I apologize to the unknown authors of both.

7. Poem from the Telegu, inscribed on a cult object now preserved in the Royal Ontario Museum, Toronto.

8. A Peter Pan view of this sort has nevertheless been seriously, not to say solemnly, urged by a leading Wittgensteinian. In a now notorious article on 'Anselm's Ontological Arguments', first published in the *Philosophical Review* for 1960, Norman Malcolm quoted from Psalm XC: "Before the mountains were brought forth, or ever Thou hadst framed the earth and the world, Thou art God." This everlasting God is, apparently, conjured into actual existence by human concerns and human language. Thus the "human phenomenon of an unbearably heavy conscience is importantly connected with the genesis of the concept of God, that is, with the formation of the 'grammar' of the word 'God' "; and "God has the status of a necessary being. Who can doubt that? Here we must say with Wittgenstein: 'This language game is played' " (Malcolm, pp. 156, 161 and 156).

9. Compare, the authority here, Popkin.

10. It is now known as his first *Inquiry*, because he also published in 1752 *An Inquiry concerning the Principles of Morals*. I shall give page references both to C. W. Hendel's edition in the Library of Liberal Arts and to L. A. Selby-Bigge's edition for the Oxford University Press. The former is by common consent in every way superior, but copies of the latter are more widely and abundantly available.

11. By far the best account of these intellectual battles is still the century-old Stephen (2). Some may draw salutary profit as well as malicious pleasure from contemplating the case of A. E. Taylor. His Sir Leslie Stephen Lecture 'David Hume and the Miraculous' made it quite clear that he had not refreshed his own memory of the very relevant work of Stephen, to which he nevertheless began by paying the usual seemly tribute (Flew (2), pp. 199–200): 'The classics are like the great. We learn their names and thereafter claim acquaintance with them.'

12. The first quotation comes from the 'Epistle to the Reader' at the beginning of Locke's *Essay*; the second is anonymous traditional, and refers to the name of Newton's college at Cambridge. The word

'philosophy' is here used in an older sense, preserved today only in the titles of our oldest chairs of physics in the fossil phrase 'natural philosophy'.

13. But those who do want to go to town sometime might start with Burtt, Chapter VII §I and or Newton, Note 55. They could then proceed, perhaps by way of Magee's excellent introduction in the Modern Masters series, to Popper (1), Part I; Popper (2), Chapter I; and Lakatos and Musgrave pp. 91–196. The phrase "bold conjectures" in the present context is, of course, Popper's.

14. See Hume's posthumously published final masterpiece *Dialogues concerning Natural Religion*, in the definitive edition of Norman Kemp Smith.

15. See Terence Penelhum's 'Divine Necessity' in *Mind* for 1960.

16. My carefully stilted words allow for the fact that this most quoted sentence is not to be found in his extant works, although there are paraphrases.

17. This paper has not yet to my knowledge been published. I am in a position to quote from it only because I happened to be one of the official respondents at that Chicago meeting.

18. For further elucidation of these curious Thomist notions see Chapter IV of Kenny, and Dr Patterson Brown's 'St. Thomas and Necessary Being' in *The Philosophical Review* for 1966. We have here one more illustration of the point that the Five Ways incorporate much more obsolete Aristotelianism than is sometimes recognised.

19. That this is indeed the desired conclusion can scarcely be denied by anyone who remembers what Aquinas had to say elsewhere *de aeternitate mundi contra murmurantes* (*Concerning the Eternity of the Universe, Against the Murmurers*) : these murmurers were those who, not then knowing that he was going to be canonised, and later to be doubly sanctified by the Encyclical *Aeterni Patris*, were accusing him of heresy. No one, on the other hand, who had to interpret this Article of the *Summa Theologica* without benefit of any other reading of Aquinas, or of good commentary, ever would, or could, or in fact does, appreciate this point. It is, though this seems too rarely to be said, most regrettable that Aquinas did not take more trouble, and allow himself more space, to make quite clear exactly what he did think he was proving here; and how.

20. Scholarship has now traced its origin back as far as the Islamic Al-Ghazali. It may well have been brought by Jesuits to France from Moorish Spain. See Miguel Palacios, *Los precedentes musulmanes del Pari de Pascal* (Santander: 1920). I thank my sometime Keele colleagues Ruth Murphy and Robert North for supplying this information, and the reference. I do not include the Palacios book in my Bibliography, because I have not been able to inspect a copy; it is not in the British Museum Library.

21. I am using the new Everyman translation, by John Warrington. I give the references by the item numbers first of the Lafuma and then of the Brunschvicg editions.

22. On the very day on which I was revising this article for republication

(15 November 1974), Mrs Margaret Knight wrote to *The Times*: "What a pity that you do not print all your news from Rome on the same page. If you had done so we could have read in today's copy side by side: '. . . urgent action to meet the threat of imminent starvation for many millions'. And 'The Pope . . . foresaw the future of women primarily as bearers of children'."

23. Compare the end of Note 4, above; and, for instance, R. J. Mostyn on 'The Damnable Doctrine' in *The Rationalist Annual* for 1959. Mostyn's title is the phrase used by Charles Darwin in his *Autobiography* as a description of the traditional hardline doctrine of damnation.

24. English-speakers should remember that the word translated 'salvation' is the normal Latin for 'safety'.

25. ". . . if anyone decides to call the sea Neptune, and corn Ceres, and to misapply the name of Bacchus rather than to give liquor its right name, so be it; and let him dub the round world 'Mother of the Gods' so long as he is careful not really to infest his mind with base superstition" (Lucretius, II, 652–657).

26. See ' "Theology and Falsification" in Retrospect' (§3 (d)), in Diamond and Litzenburg. The 'Retrospect' was originally commissioned and written as a coming of age exercise. But a series of publication delays now threatens to collapse the distinction between that and the present silver jubilee celebration.

27. The phrase "endemic evil" was perhaps unfortunate. In the summer of 1950 I happened to have very much in mind the immortality arguments of Book X of Plato's *Republic*, one of which has as a premise the thesis that everything has its *sumphuton kakon*. These congenital or endemic evils in Plato are certainly not irresistible (§§ 609A ff.).

28. Since I had made extensive oral trials in and around the Socratic Club before putting the challenge into print I was myself well aware of this diversity. See, again, the paper mentioned in Note 26 (§1). Although many did hold religious beliefs which were in principle falsifiable, no one quite matched the robust straightforwardness of Thangbrand, missionary to the Icelanders: "You heathens are to hallow one of the fires. I shall hallow the second. If the berserk is afraid of the fire I hallow, but walks unscathed through your fire, then you must accept the new faith." He was, he did, and they did: "Thangbrand asked if they would now take the new faith. Gest replied that he never made promises which he did not intend to keep. So Thangbrand baptised Gest and all his household and many others" (Magnusson and Palsson, §103).

29. Christopher Hollis nevertheless maintained that the decent virtues which Orwell cherished and championed are "logically a product of a Christian faith which Orwell rejected", and that again and again his was "clearly a position that is only tenable on the basis of a theology" (Hollis, p. 40). In a review article in *The Literary Guide*, predecessor of the now also defunct *Humanist* (London) and *New Humanist*, I argued that this is not so, and that Orwell's beliefs do not logically presuppose anything of the sort. This arguable though surely mistaken contention of Hollis must be sharply distinguished from the perverse and

preposterous stand taken by a recent American critic. This man construes the final surrender of Winston Smith biographically as Orwell's own surrender; and he can even bring himself to say of *Nineteen Eighty-four* that "only in a very superficial sense is the book talking about politics" (see *Encounter* for July 1974, pp. 70–73). I suppose that the same critic looking at D. H. Lawrence would find only a superficial interest in sex.

30. This fine formulation is in my 'Divine Omnipotence and Human Freedom' in *New Essays in Philosophical Theology* wrongly attributed to St. Augustine of Hippo (Flew and MacIntyre (Eds.), p. 144). I thank John Burnaby of Trinity College, Cambridge, for drawing my attention to my mistake. Although I am still unable to provide a precise reference, I now believe that the true source is much earlier and Epicurean, perhaps even Epicurus himself.

31. I have said a little more about these matters in the totally secular context of a discussion of Sartre's views of freedom in E. Pivcevic (Ed.) *Phenomenology and the Philosophical Understanding*.

32. 'Evil and Omnipotence' by J. L. Mackie in *Mind* 1955 and my 'Divine Omnipotence and Human Freedom', mentioned already in Note 30. A much shorter version of the latter appeared in the *Hibbert Journal* for January 1955; and it is this version, slightly corrected, which has since been reprinted in G. I. Mavrodes and S. C. Hackett (Eds.) *Perspectives in the Philosophy of Religion* and in P. Angeles (Ed.) *Modern Critical Readings in the Philosophy of Religion*. I shall refer to these two earlier articles as little as possible, in order to avoid wearisome and unprofitable 'Who-said-what-which-meant-what?' questions extending back over twenty years.

33. For an account of these ideas see Flew (4), under Creation and First Cause.

34. See, for instance, 'Dr. Clarke's First Reply' and 'Mr. Leibniz's Second Paper' in H. G. Alexander (Ed.) *The Leibniz-Clarke Correspondence*.

35. Descartes's contention was criticised by Bayle and by Leibniz. See, for instance, *Theodicy*, I, 50–51 and III, 292 ff.; and compare the discussion between C. A. Campbell, C. K. Grant, and J. J. C. Smart in *Mind* for 1951, 1952, and 1961, respectively. Schopenhauer's prize essay on *The Freedom of the Will* is especially savage about the persistence of this contention: "In Germany too there is no shortage of ignoramuses who throw to the winds all that has been said about this by great thinkers in the last 200 years, and, . . . proclaim the freedom of the will as actually given. But perhaps I am unfair to them, as it may be the case that they are not as ignorant as they seem but only hungry; and therefore, for a very dry piece of bread, teach everything that might please a lofty ministry" (Schopenhauer, p. 44).

36. Boswell's *Journal* for 10 October 1769.

37. As I have done in Flew (5), Part III.

38. For a fuller development see my 'Again the Paradigm" in P. K. Feyerabend and G. Maxwell (Eds.) *Mind, Matter, and Method*—the festschrift for Herbert Feigl.

174   NOTES

39. It is most remarkable that Plantinga is an alumnus of and a teacher at Calvin College; and that he has, it is said, out of loyalty to this alma mater refused many lucrative offers of appointments elsewhere. In spite or because of this, I have to say—not for the first nor probably for the last time—that no one has any business to plunge into print with a discussion of philosophical questions about freewill unless they have subjected themselves to the propaedeutic of some catholic course of classical reading. One good but still entirely manageable programme would be to read both Schopenhauer's prize essay and the relevant portions of all the earlier works mentioned therein.

40. This is precisely what Lady Wootton does suggest in Wootton, Chapter VIII. Compare Professor H. L. A. Hart's criticism of her approach in Hart, Chapters VII–VIII. For a masterly yet merry study of that richness of vocabulary see Austin (1), pp. 123–152.

41. In 'Hume and Historical Necessity', first read to an Oberlin Colloquium on Hume in April 1973. It is to be published, they say, by the Yale University Press in the *Proceedings* of that Colloquium, edited by N. Care.

42. See, for instance, the *Summa Theologica* III Supp. Q. 79 A2; especially the first Objection and the Reply of Aquinas.

43. See II *Kings* ii, 11 and the Papal Encyclical *Munificentissimus Deus* of 1950 (Denzinger, §§3031–3033).

44. Imagination certainly cannot be simply and generally equated with such imaging: when, for instance, we complain about unimaginative architecture we are complaining about the buildings rather than about a supposed deficiency in the inner life of their architect. See Annis Flew 'Images, Supposing, and Imagining' in *Philosophy* for 1953.

45. This phrase was originally applied, in German, to Kant. But Kant himself would surely have agreed that it sits better on the author of the *Treatise*.

46. "We could perfectly well, for our purposes, replace every process of imagining by a process of looking at an object or by painting, drawing, or modelling; and every process of speaking to oneself by speaking aloud or by writing" (Wittgenstein (3), p. 4).

47. The reference here is, of course, to the peculiarly Roman Catholic doctrine of transsubstantiation; and it is, by Hobbesian standards, mild. In Chapter XLVI he excels himself: "The Egyptian conjurers, that are said to have turned their rods to serpents, and the water into blood, are thought but to have deluded the senses of the spectators by a false show of things; yet are esteemed enchanters. But what we would have thought of them, if there had appeared in their rods nothing like a serpent, and in the water enchanted nothing like blood, nor like anything else but water; but that they had faced down the king that they were serpents that looked like rods, and that it was blood that seemed water. That was both enchantment, and lying. And yet in this daily act of the priest they do the same . . .".

48. Pierre-Henri Simon *Les Raisins Verts*, p. 97: I'm afraid I noted only the author, title and page, not the publisher.

49. See, for instance, *The Concept of Mind*, Chapter II.
50. I follow, although omitting the italics, the old translation (A.V.) rather than the new (R.V.) because the former seems here to be no less accurate, while generally it does more justice to the literary quality of the original.

BIBLIOGRAPHY

ALEXANDER, H. G. (Ed.), *The Leibniz-Clarke Correspondence* (Manchester: Manchester University Press, 1956).

ANSCOMBE, G. E. M., *An Introduction to Wittgenstein's Tractatus* (London: Hutchinson, 1959).

AQUINAS, ST. T. (1), *Summa contra Gentiles*, tr. V. J. Bourke and others (New York: Doubleday, 1956 and 1957).

AQUINAS, ST. T. (2), *Summa Theologica*, tr. The Fathers of the English Dominican Province (London: Burns Oates and Washbourne, 1920).

AUGUSTINE, ST. OF HIPPO, *St. Augustine against the Academicians*, tr. M. P. Garven (Milwaukee: Marquette University Press, 1942).

AUSTIN, J. L. (1), *Philosophical Papers* (Oxford: Clarendon Press, 1961).

AUSTIN, J. L. (2), *Sense and Sensibilia* (Oxford: Clarendon Press, 1962).

AYER, A. J., *Language, Truth and Logic* (Second Edition. London: Gollancz, 1946).

BAYLE, P., *Dictionnaire Historique et Critique* (Fourth Edition. Amsterdam and Leyden, 1730).

BERKELEY, G., *The Works of George Berkeley*, ed. A. A. Luce and T. E. Jessup (London: Nelson, 1948–1957).

BIBBY, C., *T. H. Huxley: Scientist, Humanist and Educator* (London: C. A. Watts, 1959).

BRADLEY, F. H., *Appearance and Reality* (London: Sonnenschein and New York: Macmillan, 1893).

BRAITHWAITE, R. B., *An Empiricist's View of the Nature of Religious Belief* (Cambridge: Cambridge University Press, 1955).

BURTT, E. Q., *Metaphysical Foundations of Modern Physical Science* (London: Kegan Paul and New York: Harcourt Brace, 1932).

BUTLER, J., *Butler's Works*, ed. W. E. Gladstone (Oxford: Oxford University Press, 1896).

CICERO, M. T., *de Natura Deorum, Academica*, tr. H. Rackham (London: Heinemann and Cambridge, Mass.: Harvard University Press, 1933).

CLIFFORD, W. K., *Lectures and Essays* (London: Macmillan, 1886).

COLLINGWOOD, R. G., *An Essay on Metaphysics* (Oxford: Clarendon Press, 1940).

DENZINGER, H., *Enchiridion Symbolorum* (Twenty-ninth Revised Edition. Freiberg in Breisgau: Herder, 1953).

DESCARTES, R., *Philosophical Works*, tr. E. S. Haldane and G. R. T. Ross (Cambridge: Cambridge University Press, 1931).

DIAMOND, M. and LITZENBURG, T. V. (Eds.), *The Logic of God* (Indianapolis: Bobbs-Merrill, 1975).

EDWARDS, P. (Ed.), *The Encyclopaedia of Philosophy* (New York: Macmillan and Free Press and London: Collier-Macmillan, 1967).

FEYERABEND, P. K. and MAXWELL, G. (Eds.), *Mind, Matter and Method* (Minneapolis: Minnesota University Press, 1966).

FLEW, A. G. N. (1), *A New Approach to Psychical Research* (London: C. A. Watts, 1953).

FLEW, A. G. N. (2), *Hume's Philosophy of Belief* (London: Routledge and Kegan Paul and New York: Philosophical Library, 1961).

FLEW, A. G. N. (3), *God and Philosophy* (London: Hutchinson and New York: Harcourt Brace, 1966).

FLEW, A. G. N. (4), *An Introduction to Western Philosophy* (London: Thames and Hudson and Indianapolis: Bobbs-Merrill, 1971).

FLEW, A. G. N. (5), *Crime or Disease?* (London: Macmillan and New York: Barnes and Noble, 1973).

FLEW, A. G. N. (Ed.) (1), *Logic and Language* (Oxford: Blackwell, First Series 1951).

FLEW, A. G. N. (Ed.) (2), *Logic and Language* (Oxford: Blackwell, Second Series 1953).

FLEW, A. G. N. and MACINTYRE, A. C. (Eds.), *New Essays in Philosophical Theology* (London: Student Christian Movement, 1955).

HART, H. L. A., *Punishment and Responsibility* (Oxford: Clarendon Press, 1968).

HAWKINS, G. and MORRIS, N., *The Honest Politician's Guide to Crime Control* (Chicago: Chicago University Press, 1970).

HEIMBECK, R. S., *Theology and Meaning* (London: Allen and Unwin, 1969).

HICK, J. R. (Ed.), *Classical and Contemporary Readings in the Philosophy of Religion* (Englewood Cliffs, N.J.: Prentice-Hall, 1970).

HOLLIS, C., *A Study of George Orwell* (London: Hollis and Carter, 1956).

HUME, D. (1), *A Treatise of Human Nature*, ed. L. A. Selby-Bigge (Oxford: Oxford University Press, 1906).

HUME, D. (2), *An Inquiry concerning Human Understanding*, ed. C. W. Hendel (New York: Liberal Arts, 1955).

HUME, D. (3), *An Inquiry concerning the Principles of Morals*, ed. C. W. Hendel (New York: Liberal Arts, 1957).

HUME, D. (4), *The Natural History of Religion*, ed. H. E. Root (London: A. and C. Black, 1956).

HUME, D. (5), *Dialogues concerning Natural Religion*, ed. N. Kemp Smith (Second Edition. Edinburgh: Nelson, 1947).

HUXLEY, T. H. (1), *Hume: with helps to the study of Berkeley* (London: Macmillan, 1894).

HUXLEY, T. H. (2), *Collected Essays* (London: Macmillan, 1904).

KANT, I. (1), *Critique of Pure Reason*, tr. N. Kemp Smith (London: Macmillan, 1929).

KANT, I. (2), *Critique of Practical Reason*, tr. L. W. Beck (New York: Library of Liberal Arts, 1956).

KENNY, A., *The Five Ways* (London: Routledge and Kegan Paul and New York: Schocken, 1969).

LAKATOS, I. and MUSGRAVE, A. (Eds.), *Criticism and the Growth of Knowledge* (Cambridge: Cambridge University Press, 1970).

LEIBNIZ, G. W., *Theodicy*, tr. E. M. Huggard (London: Routledge and Kegan Paul, 1951).

LEIBNIZ, G. W., *Leibniz Selections*, ed. P. P. Wiener (New York: Scribner, 1951).

LENIN, V. I., *Materialism and Empirio-Criticism* (Moscow: Foreign Languages Publishing House, 1952).

LOCKE, J., *An Essay concerning Human Understanding*, ed. A. C. Fraser (Oxford: Oxford University Press, 1894).

LUCAS, J. R., *The Freedom of the Will* (Oxford: Clarendon Press, 1970).

LUCRETIUS, T. C., *de Rerum Natura*, tr. W. D. H. Rouse (London: Heinemann and Cambridge, Mass.: Harvard University Press, 1947).

LUTHER, M., *The Bondage of the Will*, tr. J. I. Packer and O. R. Johnston (London: J. Clarke, 1957).

MACINTYRE, A. C. (Ed.), *Metaphysical Beliefs* (London: Student Christian Movement, 1957).

MAGEE, B., *Popper* (London: Collins/Fontana, 1973).

MAGNUSSON, M. and PALSSEN, H. (Tr.), *Njal's Saga* (Harmondsworth: Penguin, 1960).

MALCOLM, N., *Knowledge and Certainty* (Englewood Cliffs, N.J.: Prentice-Hall, 1963).

MANSEL, H., *The Limits of Religious Thought* (London: Oxford University Press, 1858).

MARTIN, C. B., *Religious Belief* (Ithaca, N.Y.: Cornell University Press, 1959).

MOHAMMED, The Prophet, *The Koran*, tr. N. J. Dawood (Harmondsworth: Penguin, 1956).

MOTTRAM, V. H., *The Physical Basis of Personality* (Harmondsworth: Penguin, 1944).

NEWTON, I., *Newton's Principia*, ed. F. Cajori (Berkeley: University of California Press, 1946).

ORWELL, G. (1), *Animal Farm* (London: Secker and Warburg, 1945).

ORWELL, G. (2), *Nineteen Eighty-four* (London: Secker and Warburg, 1949).

PASCAL, B., *Pensées*, tr. J. Warrington (London: Dent and New York: Dutton, 1960).

PEIRCE, C. S., *Collected Papers* (Cambridge, Mass.: Harvard University Press, 1934 onwards).

PENELHUM, T., *Survival and Disembodied Existence* (London: Routledge and Kegan Paul and New York: Humanities Press, 1970).

PIVCEVIC, E. (Ed.), *Phenomenology and the Philosophical Understanding* (Cambridge: Cambridge University Press, 1975).

PLANTINGA, A., *God and Other Minds* (Ithaca, N.Y.: Cornell University Press, 1967).

PLATO, *The Laws*, tr. R. G. Bury (London: Heinemann and Cambridge, Mass.: Harvard University Press, 1952).

POPKIN, R. H., *The History of Scepticism from Erasmus to Descartes* (Assen, Netherlands: Van Gorcum, 1960).

POPPER, K. R. (1), *The Logic of Scientific Discovery* (London: Hutchinson, 1959).

POPPER, K. R. (2), *Conjectures and Refutations* (London: Routledge and Kegan Paul, 1963).

REID, T., *Essays on the Intellectual Powers of Man*, ed. A. D. Worzley (London: Macmillan, 1941).

RHINE, J. B. (1), *New Frontiers of the Mind* (Harmondsworth: Penguin, 1950).

RHINE, J. B. (2), *The Reach of the Mind* (Harmondsworth: Penguin, 1954).

RUSSELL, B. A. W. (1), *Our Knowledge of the External World* (London: Allen and Unwin, 1914).

RUSSELL, B. A. W. (2), *Introduction to Mathematical Philosophy* (London: Allen and Unwin, 1919).

RYLE, G., *The Concept of Mind* (London: Hutchinson, 1949).

SCHOPENHAUER, A., *The Freedom of the Will*, tr. K. Kolenda (Indianapolis: Bobbs-Merrill, 1960).

SMYTHIES, J. R. (Ed.), *Brain and Mind* (London: Routledge and Kegan Paul and New York: Humanities Press, 1965).

STEPHEN, L. (1), *An Agnostic's Apology, and Other Essays* (London: C. A. Watts, 1931).

STEPHEN, L. (2), *English Thought in the Eighteenth Century* (Reproduction of the Third Edition of 1902. New York: P. Smith, 1949).

STRAWSON, P. F. (1), *An Introduction to Logical Theory* (London: Methuen, 1952).

STRAWSON, P. F. (2), 'Persons' in H. Feigl, M. Scriven, and G. Maxwell (Eds.), *Minnesota Studies in the Philosophy of Science: II Concepts,*

Theories and the Mind-Body Problem (Minneapolis: Minnesota University Press, 1958).

STRAWSON, P. F. (3), *Individuals* (London: Methuen, 1959).

TERTULLIAN, *de Anima*, in Part II of *Tertulliani Opera*, ed. J. M. Clément (Turnhout, Belgium: Brepols, 1954).

TOLSTOY, L. N. (1), *A Confession*, tr. A. Maude (London and New York: Oxford University Press, 1940).

TOLSTOY, L. N. (2), *Works*, tr. A. Maude (London: Milford, 1929).

TYRRELL, G. N. M., *Apparitions* (London: Duckworth, 1953).

URMSON, J. O. (Ed.), *A Concise Encyclopaedia of Philosophy and Philosophers* (London: Hutchinson, 1960).

WELLS, H. G., *The Invisible Man* (Harmondsworth: Penguin, 1946).

WISDOM, J., *Other Minds* (Oxford: Blackwell, 1952).

WITTGENSTEIN, L. (1), *Tractatus Logico-Philosophicus*, tr. C. K. Ogden (London: Kegan Paul and New York: Harcourt Brace, 1923).

WITTGENSTEIN, L. (2), *Philosophical Investigations*, tr. G. E. M. Anscombe (Oxford: Blackwell, 1953).

WITTGENSTEIN, L. (3), *The Blue and the Brown Books* (Oxford: Blackwell, 1958).

WOOTTON, B., *Social Science and Social Pathology* (London: Allen and Unwin, 1959).

YOUNG, A. F. and ASHTON, E. T., *British Social Work in the Nineteenth Century* (London: Routledge and Kegan Paul, 1956).

Index of Names

This is intended to cover the notes as well as the text, but to exclude the names of both Gods and fictitious, legendary or mythological persons.